THE SHAPELESS GOD

THE SHAPE- LESS GOD

Essays on Modern Fiction

Harry J. Mooney, Jr.

AND

Thomas F. Staley

EDITORS

University of Pittsburgh Press

65005

Library of Congress Catalog Card Number 68–21630
SBN 8229-3161-3
Copyright © 1968, University of Pittsburgh Press
Manufactured in the United States of America
Second Printing, 1969

To the memory of
Fabian R. Staley
and
Harry J. Mooney

Preface

I don't suppose any church would accept me, but I believe in
God and His grace with an absolute confidence. It is by his grace
that we know beauty and love. . . . Without that belief I could
not make sense of the world and I could not write. . . . God is a
character, a real and consistent being, or he is nothing.

—*Joyce Cary*

Joyce Cary's words form a kind of epigraph for the essays in this book, each of which attempts to analyze specific components of what may be regarded as the religious awareness—a set of particular attitudes toward God and the question of man's relationship to Him—of the writer it is considering. Although theology, ranging from a rather informal to a quite formal kind, necessarily enters some of these discussions, it does so primarily in a literary context. At issue here is the complex, demanding problem of defining the way in which, in a given work of art, religious attitudes are dramatized and thus revealed.

Long before Christianity, writers and other artists saw man primarily in relation to gods or God. It would be simplistic, and therefore rash, to suppose that this relationship is any less relevant in the world of modern literature; indeed, the very concept of the Death of God, although an inversion of the traditional religious postulate, can hardly be regarded as merely or only secular. At the same time, it nevertheless projects what have long been questions the answers to which were sought at least partially in the supernatural realm into far more specifically temporal dimensions: the meaning of man's life, in the most exalted sense of his natural desire to achieve meaning, must be worked out in terms of that life *alone*, and of his relationship to the events and situations external to him. At the same time, writers with more orthodox religious beliefs have tended to follow one of two alternatives: they may, like Ignazio Silone, as his development is traced in the essay by Robert McAfee Brown, hold, often quite fiercely, to established Christian concepts and be concerned to show how, in the modern world, these concepts are preserved outside of institutions and churches (often, of course, because churches *are* institutions), or they may, like Flannery O'Connor, use a set of quite orthodox religious convictions as the material of an art so unorthodox in form and vision as to yield fiction entirely original in kind. Perhaps the greatest strength, from a literary point of view, of fiction which is overtly religious in its concern is that it is seldom derivative: the ferment of contemporary religion, on the one hand, and the constant search for new forms in fiction, on the other, operate conclusively against the conventions.

The following questions, then, are perhaps in order in an introduction to the present volume, for one or another of them stands at the heart of every essay: How does an awareness of the eternal and of its penetration into the temporal (in the sense in which this theme is treated, with full consciousness of its complexity, in Eliot's later poetry) manifest itself in specific works of the writer under discussion? What are the consequences of this awareness for the writer's sense of the meaning and purpose of life, and how does it shape his vision of human relations and experiences? What, following upon this last question, is the basic equation of religious vision and literary form? If a writer's positions are relatively orthodox, his applications are, of course, more easily grasped; yet a writer like Graham Greene proves how precarious may be the connection between an allegiance to orthodox belief on the one hand, and the way in which religious values assert themselves in fiction on the other. In the case of the less orthodox, or totally unorthodox, the problem, of course, grows vastly more complex, and questions of definition arise on every level. What, then, whether orthodox or otherwise, are the religious assumptions upon which the works of these writers are based? And, ultimately and most significantly, how can these assumptions be defined, and then be demonstrated in operation, *within the works themselves?*

Within the boundaries of the last question, delimited in formulation, yet endlessly expansive in application, lies the true distinction to be drawn between literary criticism and theological argument. The primary task of all nine contributors to this volume has therefore been to define a writer's religious vision as the determining component of his work, with the concomitant obligation to analyze the way in which such a vision is dramatized. Literature, after all, is a kind of vast metaphor; and if the writer's art first demands that he *dramatize* his values within the endlessly complex and inconclusive metaphors presented by human experience, the critic's primary task is to comment on his work in terms of this recognition.

The rationale behind the present volume is, the editors hope, simultaneously eclectic and unifying. The writers discussed obviously represent a variety of approaches to religious experience, and each has his unique method of communicating it within the self-sustaining organism of a work of art. No particular essay (nor the book as a whole, either by any totality of design or by more indirect methods) bears the burden of the need to arrive at broadly inclusive statements; some essays do, however, study a writer's work in general, while focussing on some parts of it more than others, and some center immediately on works regarded as characteristic. One quality all the essays share: they are dedicated rather exclusively to the writers they examine. Of genuine concern on all occasions has been the desire to provide a valid study of one *x*   author rather than an explication of general movements or of a writer's relationship to these movements. Even here, though, there are partial exceptions; Mr. Staley's study of Coccioli, certainly the least known of these writers to an American audience, has been placed first in the book precisely because it attempts to do more with significant questions of general background than do the others.

HARRY J. MOONEY, JR.
THOMAS F. STALEY

Contents

Contents

THE SHAPELESS GOD

Thomas F. Staley

Faith and the Absurd: The Post-Existential Vision of Carlo Coccioli

No, no, Lazarus. You are wrong.
Your truth is not the Truth.
—Miguel De Unamuno

According to Georg Lukács, the central aesthetic problem of realism is the adequate presentation of the complete human personality in a work of art. The novelists of the twentieth century, whether in the symbolism of Joyce, the surrealism of Kafka, or the artistic design of Gide, have struggled to render this complete human personality—this personality in an age of lost values, lost men, and lost gods.

The history of the novel from Richardson and Fielding to Dostoevsky, Joyce, and Camus reveals the essential truth of Lukács' observation. Whether the character in a novel is Tom Jones, Ivan Karamazov, or Leopold Bloom, he must in some way relate to the universe around him and even beyond him (examples of the latter would be Ivan Karamazov's recitation of the Legend of the Grand Inquisitor, or, at another extreme,

4 Leopold Bloom's fantasies in the Circe episode of *Ulysses*). Fiction in the nineteenth century grew out of the social and moral problems created by a rapidly expanding and changing world, and from its humble beginnings it has been saturated with social and moral humanistic problems. The novel grew in stature because it was the literary genre best able to express the realities of human and ideological conflict. But more than any other literary form, it has also been more susceptible to the changing course of events and ideas in history. Out of the holocaust of two great wars in this century there emerged in the continental novel a myriad of new currents of thought, the most dominant being a profound sense of nothingness and of the deterioration in human relationships. This development was not necessarily an abandonment of past values, but a concept deeply rooted in Hegel, Nietzsche, and Kierkegaard. At the same time, this concept retained its own character, and was shaped by the events as much as by the ideas of history. The shadow of this thought (especially as it expresses itself in literature) and all of its mutations cannot be put under the shadow of one tree and called existentialism, for quite obviously each generation and each writer within that generation views the world in a different way.[1] But serious novelists ever since World War II have had to recognize, as Richard Chase has clearly pointed out, "the high, tense world of strenuous and difficult metaphysics . . . and religious feeling."[2] In other words, they have had to confront the terror that men of our age feel in the face of spiritual nullity on the one hand and the possibility of total self-annihilation on the other.

Whether an author is a believer or non-believer, his confrontation with nothingness and absurdity can be expressed in any number of ways—in black comedy, or in the variety of modern expressions of non-tragedy (my own term). For all its seeming pessimism, this imagination, whether it be called atheistic existentialism, neo-Christian existentialism, or by

any other name, can probe deeply into the human consciousness, and if brilliantly conceived and executed, it will like all
art offer up a mirror to man and give him a picture of himself
and his age.[3]

The entire syndrome of European existentialism after World
War II (with the large and interesting exception of Gabriel
Marcel) expressed itself in terms of the individual alienated or
removed from any supernatural source. Until recently this expression of thought, with all its obvious variations, dominated
the literature of post-World War II Europe. But, as is always
the case with the novel, new currents of thought have sprung
in various directions. As existential thought spreads in a
variety of directions, one intriguing question arises: What of
the novelists who have admitted this sense of absurdity in
human life and try not to beg the questions, but who still accept the belief in a God who is the source of human faith and
hope? And what of the novelist who—perhaps with greater
difficulty—asks how the Church confronts man in his moral
and metaphysical estrangement in an absurd world? Does the
Church merely dictate a system whereby one can become a
saint, martyr, or sinner? It is within the context of these questions that the serious novelist who writes of moral and spiritual matters finds himself.

The concept of God and man's relationship to God has
obviously undergone radical changes. It is difficult enough to
attempt to portray honestly the shapelessness and absurdity
of life in the twentieth century, but to deal in this light with the
problem of faith, the conflict between orthodoxy and faith,
man's relationship with God, what it means metaphysically
to be a believer, what it means to be without faith in God—all
of this seems next to impossible. To find the dramatic terms in
which to present this conflict in art is the great task of the contemporary novelist who wishes to explore this profound and
complex mystery.

6   This is not to say that it is any less difficult to recognize the prodigious senselessness of things, the absurdity of the world, than it is to commit what Camus called "philosophical suicide," to renounce reason and leap to hope. According to Camus, it is the absurd man who is able to recognize that his truth is not the truth (as Unamuno says). It is the absurd man, too, Camus believes, who is able to stand consciously face to face with irrationality and nothingness. Camus' great contribution to modern thought (and more especially, literature) has been assessed extremely well by Leon F. Seltzer. In a recent article Seltzer writes: "Camus' contribution to the literature of the absurd lies mainly in his descriptions of what he terms 'the absurd man' and 'the absurd creation.' As far as his recognition of an absurd universe is concerned, there is, of course, nothing original in his thinking."[4] Because of his concern with the individual (a concern far different from Sartre's), as well as with the human personality confronted with an absurd universe, Camus' philosophy and writings have exerted an enormous influence on younger European novelists. Camus revitalizes once again the dramatic interplay between the human personality and its relationship to the totality which surrounds but does not enslave him.[5]

The direction of Camus' thought has provided an excellent springboard for those later novelists who occupy themselves with the contradictions suggested in his writings. More importantly, and closer to the aim of this essay, is the fact that Camus' art and his ideas concerning human existence have been important influences on novelists who have dealt with serious religious themes. These novelists have tried to be no less equivocal than Camus, but they see in the face of absurdity the double token of faith.[6] Upon recognizing the absurd, they seem to insist, one can also recognize the Divine—perhaps never again in orthodoxy or conventional religious terms, but in the God the late Paul Tillich writes of in *The*

Courage to Be: "The ultimate source of the courage to be is the 'God above God'; this is the result of our demand to transcend theism. Only if the God of theism is transcended can the anxiety of doubt and meaninglessness be taken into the courage to be."

The time has passed when the believer can write with that assurance about God that Claudel proclaimed so bombastically in his letters to Gide. The other extreme, which insists that God is dead, can be viewed in the hysterical proclamations, convoluted syntax, and rather superficial but arrogant assurance of a theologian such as Thomas J. J. Altizer. At either extreme lie dangers.

The serious novelist of today who attempts to deal with theological and religious problems must take into account the powerful, agonizingly beautiful vision of man that has been given to him by Kierkegaard and, more especially, Camus. In the light of contemporary man's questions about his universe, he must, as Tillich says, "mediate a courage which takes doubt and meaninglessness into itself." The clearest example of an emergence of a new conscience forged by post-World War II thinking can be found in the British novelist Graham Greene. Greene, who dealt in his early novels with conventional if not orthodox religious themes, has since moved to the treatment of existential and far more broadly human problems. *A Burnt-Out Case* was the transitional novel; his latest novel, *The Comedians*, illustrates the progress of his evolution. But younger novelists than Greene, novelists who began writing only after World War II, have been deeply concerned with the question of faith in a world which to all outward and even inward appearances has seemed meaningless. The fiction of the Italian novelist Carlo Coccioli offers an excellent illustration of the post-existential novelist who has tried to integrate existential thought with unorthodox Christian idealism (unorthodox in terms of the institutional Roman Catholic

8   Church). Coccioli in his fiction attempts to deal with the problems of faith in the light of the existential philosophy exemplified by Camus.

II

I often ask myself why a Christian instinct frequently draws
me more to the religionless than to the religious. . . .

—Dietrich Bonhoeffer

Carlo Coccioli was born in Livorno, spent time in Africa, and took part in the Italian Resistance during World War II. Since then he has spent long periods of time in Florence, Paris, and Mexico. In spite of certain natural affinities with Moravia and Silone, Coccioli is distinctly removed from the mainstream of Italian literature. Two subjects pervade his fiction: homosexuality and religion. The two vie with each other, both substantively and thematically, but religion is by far the stronger. Except for Dostoevsky, who is a major influence on his work, the tradition from which Coccioli's fiction derives is almost totally French. His fiction seems a curious mixture of Huysmans, Gide, Bernanos, Mauriac, and Camus. (Since Coccioli's later novels have been written in French instead of Italian, his affinity with French writers is not merely thematic.) Certainly, his sensibility and his concept of the Catholic Church are far more closely allied to French thought than to Italian.

The chief weakness of Coccioli's fiction prior to *The White Stone*[7] is his inability to assimilate and fuse the various themes which run throughout his work. His earlier fiction is further weakened by a dependence on a superstitious and nearly hyssterical sense of faith, coupled with a shrill outcry at the evil of the modern world. Earlier novels like *Manuel the Mexican* suffer from the author's inability to separate himself from involvement and from distracting comment on the religious experiences of his characters. His technical devices and contraptions, such as letters, newspaper accounts, and diaries, fail to give the illusion of objectivity. Coccioli's vision comes dangerously close to being narrow, dogmatic, and tractarian, and relies upon miracles, mysterious divine communications, and shamanistic phenomena. The inner structure and organizational patterns of both *Manuel the Mexican* and *Heaven and Earth* barely miss being hollow imitations of journeys to Christian sainthood. It is not until *The White Stone* that material and theme begin to fuse into an excellent work of art. The spiritual fire of a Bernanos, the search and doubt of a Camus, the worldly sense of a Gide, as well as Coccioli's own unique contribution, are combined in this novel. Still, for all their failures, Coccioli's earlier novels portray vividly the sense of man's struggle with the spiritual elements in his life.

In *Manuel the Mexican* Coccioli takes up the essential themes with which all his fiction will later deal, although the treatment will then be different. Another important aspect of this novel is its interesting treatment of the absorption of the Aztec gods into the Mexican soul and the way in which these primitive vestiges still remain in spite of years of Christian domination. The denouement of the novel, however, is far too melodramatic, and the protagonist's search seems to be primarily for theological conclusions rather than for love and wisdom, as may be supposed.

Heaven and Earth presents a character who attempts to come to terms with the "worldly and unworldly," the spirit and the intellect, the emotions and the senses; but he does so in purely conventional religious terms, always within the framework of the institutional Church. The hero of the novel, the priest Don Ardito Piccardi (later to reappear in *The White Stone*), tries to come to grips with all of the conflicting elements in his life. Unfortunately, the character of the priest at the beginning of this novel seems erratically conceived. Even more seriously, the great themes of sainthood and martyrdom inspire in the novel-

10 ist nothing more than tired theological clichés and a queasiness over social concern. The blessings of sorrow and suffering, the emotional mass, miracles, absurd and reactionary theology are not enough, however, to destroy this novel completely. Strangely enough, *Heaven and Earth* gets stronger as it goes on; the first part of the novel is extremely weak, but the character of the priest becomes a better and better figure; Coccioli seems more and more sure of his ground, less drifting, more artful. By the end of the novel he has created a moving and real figure, but one far different from the character present at the novel's opening. Don Ardito emerges as a vivid character who struggles against the forces and events which play havoc with his soul and mind. Just as Don Ardito grows in strength, so too does the novel itself seem to gain in precision. The questions Don Ardito begins to ask have far more significance, and are no longer merely culled from rote memory—more important, they no longer derive from ultraconservative theologians or the Italian Christian Democratic Party. As Andrei Sinyavsky has written: "It is sometimes said that a writer has no obligation to 'solve' anything. He need only 'pose' the questions of the time, leaving the answers to his generation, to society and history." But, Sinyavsky goes on to write, "to 'pose' questions means more than to name them. . . ."[8] Although in *Heaven and Earth* Coccioli continues to seek solutions to his questions, he somewhere stops trying to answer them according to canon law. *Heaven and Earth* may suffer from the inevitable uneasiness of a writer desperately in search of something new and different and still reluctant to strike out on his own, but it dramatically illustrates the tensions and the growth in a novelist evolving from a conventional and neat (but undistinguished) religious writer to one seriously and honestly probing the spiritual life of man in the twentieth century.

In the novel that follows *Heaven and Earth*, *The White Stone*, Coccioli's real talent emerges, and he moves away from his role as a defender of the status quo and the Church to become an explorer of modern spiritual values. But Coccioli is never at peace, and all of his later novels reveal this unrelenting tension between longing for God and yearning for freedom from Him.

III

This is the significance of the first question in the wilderness, and this is what Thou hast rejected for the sake of that freedom which Thou hast exalted above everything. Yet in this question lies hid the great secret of this world. . . .

—Fyodor Dostoevsky

Although *The White Stone* explores man's dilemma in a world without God, Coccioli is not without the vision of an older order, and in this respect he is like Mauriac or Graham Greene.[9] In a specifically Catholic sense, writers such as the early Greene, Mauriac, and Bernanos are concerned with the sacramental life; while they are not pious or smug, they yearn nostalgically for the lost age of faith. The most beautiful visions of their heroes are of the rich history of the Church of the past. The hero in one of Greene's novels yearns for an older Church, an "underground" Church, a persecuted Church, able to be pure once again. Mauriac's aspiring seminarian in *The Lamb* speaks of his faith in the imagery of battle, praying "that a day would come, please God, when he would emerge from his Novitiate fortified and armed against all such snares, when this gift of his, finally sublimated, would be to him as a weapon with which to achieve the conquest of Grace." No, Coccioli is not without these visions, but his approach is far different; Don Ardito Piccardi, the hero of *The White Stone*, is also forced to see the world from the other side of the coin, from the absurd viewpoint of a Camus or a Kierkegaard. He must look at the world without any hope in Divine Redemption. If he equivocates, it is only at the last dramatic moment; only after all else has been explored, is he able to say "I be-

12   lieve!" But even after he has said "I believe," his life does not
end by searching for God, longing for salvation, and finding
redemption in morality. In *The White Stone*, as in the work of
Beckett and Camus, the good and the bad, the believers and
non-believers alike, find themselves in an absurd world.

The hero of *The White Stone* is a Catholic priest who loses
his faith and regains it, but the circumstances of his loss of
faith and subsequent alienation from God give us a striking
portrait of a man who has entered both worlds. On the one
hand, Don Ardito is acutely aware of his responsibility to his
fellow man in a universe which is clearly absurd and in which
man is merely an accident. On the other hand, he is con-
tinuously haunted by a strong religious vision which is indelibly Christian and sacramental. Coccioli's hero is not a split
personality, nor does he try to make both worlds compatible.
The world without faith that he experiences is much more
illuminating for him because in it he sees his essential responsibility as a man; his ultimate acceptance of God is all the
more meaningful for what he has been. It is in the incomprehensible universe, without a first cause and with all its absurdity, that Don Ardito ultimately finds unity with man and
with God.

Camus once called religion intellectual suicide. He went on
to say that religion provides man with a false sense of security
in an essentially absurd world, and if a man takes on a Christian philosophy which views the world as only a temporary
disorder, after which everything will make sense, he begins to
abdicate his human responsibilities. Existentialism is a philosophy of disorientation; Christianity presupposes a philosophy
of orientation. Don Ardito, content in his faith and willing to
die for the young Italian guerrillas in the name of his priesthood, sees only a world of order, even in death, until he loses
his faith. Later he writes in his diary: "I have to admit that the
world did not collapse the moment I felt that God did not exist.
I must also admit that the things which I thought inextricably

linked to God and dependent upon Him exist in themselves,
the destruction of God did not provoke their destruction. The only consequence of the death of God is that they become incomprehensible."

Torn from the original meaning of his existence, Don Ardito sets out on a spiritual journey, or quest, into a world where the supernatural or divine no longer has any meaning.

World War II and its aftermath are appropriate backgrounds for a man's loss of faith. Captain Rauch, the German officer who refuses to give Don Ardito his martyrdom, arranges for a mock execution by firing squad after he has been captured, so that Don Ardito's friends will believe him martyred for the cause: Rauch then has him sent away secretly to a concentration camp. Surrounded by medieval symbols of the older Church in an Italian castle, Don Ardito is blindfolded (symbolic of his blind faith) and lined up to be shot. The shots ring out—

Then silence. In that silence a strange thing happened: I
was enveloped by the smell of blood, as if I had been led through
a slaughterhouse. But it was my own smell, and I knew it. Someone
told me once that I smelled of blood. I never realized it until
that moment. In the silence that followed the firing I knew that I
had always smelled of blood, ever since birth. Then another
strange thing happened: I moved. I made a barely perceptible
movement, but I made it. And there I was, leaning against a wall
in that court yard in the pale light of dawn, and terribly cold.
A question rose up inside me, a question: What am I doing here?
Suddenly I had a new and frightening awareness of time and place,
but in that new dimension there was something missing. There
was a dark pit. A moment before it had been filled by God.
A moment later there was only an emptiness.

It is from this dramatic moment, when God is suddenly drained from him, that Don Ardito's journey begins. His condition echoes Rilke's words from *Der Ölbaumgarten*:

> I am alone with all man's grief,
> which I tried to heal through Thee,
> Thou who art not. O nameless shame. . . .

The quest for meaning without God takes Don Ardito to the ends of the earth: Eastern Europe, France, Mexico, and back to Italy. The world becomes an absurd vacuum. Camus defines the absurd as the conjunction of man's need for an explanation and reality's inability to give one. Sartre in *La Nausée* suggests that things exist gratuitously, without cause, in defiance of reason—this is the world that Don Ardito explores after God has ceased to have meaning for him. His quest brings him into contact with a bizarre cast of characters: the "Commando" priests in France; Augustan Nevers, who under Don Ardito's influence becomes a priest in spite of Don Ardito's insistence that there is no God; Mr. Page, the archetype of Satan; and a series of characters from out of the Godless Europe of the Fifties.

C. (Coccioli himself), the figure in the novel who pieces together from interviews, diaries, and letters Don Ardito's life after his loss of belief, is at first a reluctant detective. He asks early in the novel, "That Lazarus, what does he want from me?"

Significantly enough, from the outset C. identifies Don Ardito as a Lazarus figure, an appropriate archetype for twentieth century wanderers—the Biblical man who was raised from the dead and who lives on the Mount of Olives. The Lazarus theme is an interesting and recurring one in modern Italian fiction. Moravia uses it in *Two Women*, and Silone names the enduring peasant in *A Handful of Blackberries* Lazarus.

Don Ardito Piccardi is the modern Lazarus, without faith, love, or community—the alienated man. Alienated from his fellow man and from his priesthood, but destined to bear witness for a God in whom he no longer believes, he is the man who has encountered nothingness, who is utterly disengaged and empty. Throughout the novel there are continual references to Don Ardito's malaise, his thirst, his sallow face, his distant and preoccupied stare—all characteristics of the Lazarus archetype. The priest's experiences with death in Italy and at the concentration camp, his rejection of God, his painful hegira in Eastern Europe, his shooting in Mexico, are all facets of Coccioli's portrayal of the modern Lazarus figure. And Lazarus is also, of course, a figure of human resurrection.

But like Pär Lagerkvist in his tetralogy, Coccioli insists upon a moral consideration—Don Ardito must continually bear witness to man's plight. He must search for something beyond survival, something compatible with resurrection and immortality. He is forced to do so in a world "conceived like a machine which would not function without its engine." Like Lazarus, naked and desolate, Don Ardito must explore the mystery handed to him from Chapter II of the Apocalypse, which is intricately tied to the theme of the novel: "To him that conquereth, I will give the hidden manna, and I will give a white stone, and upon the stone a new name written which no one knoweth, except him that receiveth it."

Along the way Don Ardito is tempted by many varieties of experience, but he realizes that he must transcend mysticism if he is to find God again; it, too, becomes meaningless to him in his search. In his rejection of mysticism for involvement in the world, Don Ardito offers a clear illustration of what Paul Tillich is talking about in *The Courage to Be*: "Mysticism does not take seriously the concrete and the doubt concerning the concrete. It plunges directly into the ground of being and meaning, and leaves the concrete, the world of finite values and meanings, behind. Therefore, it does not solve the problem of meaninglessness." Perhaps Don Ardito never fully solves the problem of meaninglessness, but he does recognize the necessity of action and commitment in an essentially meaningless world. His action is solidly grounded in human love, but his decisions are necessarily difficult ones.

The full cycle of Don Ardito's faith, loss of faith, and return is completed in a church near a lonely Mexican village: he is

16 shot and nearly killed while harboring young Profiro Galvan from Antonio Rodriguez and his men, who are trying to kill the young boy. Don Ardito picks up an ugly iron cross from the altar of the Blessed Virgin, walks out of the small church of Malpan with the cross held high in his right hand, and shouts "God!" He is immediately felled by two shots, but Rodriguez and his men flee, leaving the boy they had set out to kill. Don Ardito falls in the Mexican dust: "When he opened his eyes, his first words were 'I want to confess.' " This scene stands in direct contrast to the sham execution at the castle.

These two scenes, with their similar sacrifice and willing death, are in dramatic opposition to each other. The first results in Don Ardito's loss of faith, the second in his faith regained. In the castle, Don Ardito is all too willing to die blindfolded; content with his martyrdom, his thoughts of God and miracles place him in a mystical state far removed from the needs and wants of men. He is at peace with God and the world; he can accept the disorder and chaos of a war-torn world as God's will. He stands ready to die like a medieval Crusader, untouched by the longing of men.

The scene in the courtyard of the little church holds far different implications. Coccioli here insists that man's needs are not answered in the Church alone. Don Ardito takes the cross from the church and bears it out among men. Symbolically enough, it is this dramatic bearing of the cross outside of the church that climaxes Don Ardito's recognition of his priestly mission—but not before he has experienced a long night of Gethsemane in the lonely church with the young Mexican, who reveals his own wandering search and lost heritage as a halfbreed cut off from both cultures.

Don Ardito's profound Christian affirmation at the end of the novel is not without its echo of ambiguity, for the priest dies alone and obscure, never able to reveal the message on the white stone. The message remains a private symbol, a symbol for all men to ponder—the answers of faith are private and not universal, Coccioli seems to insist. In *The White Stone* there is no superimposition of the author's theological resolution upon the drama. As in *Billy Budd*, the Christian reconciliation in Coccioli's novel is not clear-cut; it remains for the reader to ponder the strange life of Don Ardito Piccardi, whose existential conviction seemed to lay as strong a claim on him as his Christian faith.

NOTES

1. A good example of the distinctions that can be drawn between writers of two generations is the one that R. W. B. Lewis makes in his *Picaresque Saint* (see bibliography). He distinguishes between the "artistic" world of Proust, Joyce, and Mann and the "human" world of Moravia, Silone, Camus, Faulkner, Greene, and Malraux. Each of these latter six writers is different from one another, but certain general yet perceptive statements can be made about them collectively.

2. Richard Chase, *The Democratic Vista* (New York, 1958), p. 16.

3. One must, of course, note the seemingly obvious but necessary reminder of Wayne C. Booth that the very worst works of art can embody the most noble themes. *The Rhetoric of Fiction* (Chicago, 1961), p. 32.

4. Leon F. Seltzer, "Camus's Absurd and the World of Melville's *Confidence-Man*," PMLA, LXXXII (March 1967), p. 15. Also see footnote seven (7) on the same page.

5. There still remain those novelists who ignore the implications or reject completely the ideas which have dominated serious thinking for the past forty years. An excellent example of this rejection may be found in the French novel, *The New Priests*, by Michel de Saint Pierre (Herder and Herder). This novel is nothing more than a reactionary diatribe against all modern movements within the Church, the characters being merely puppets who express the various arguments against these modern movements.

6. For an excellent discussion of Camus in the context of the Catholic Church, see Thomas Merton, "Albert Camus and the Church," *The Catholic Worker*, XXXIII (December 1966).

7. The three novels under discussion in this essay and the dates when

18 they were published in America are as follows (these are not the original publication dates):
   Heaven and Earth, Prentice-Hall, Inc., 1952.
   Manuel the Mexican, Simon and Schuster, 1958.
   The White Stone, Simon and Schuster, 1960.

   8. Andrei Sinyavsky, *Encounter,* April, 1967.
   9. Part of this section appeared in a slightly different form in *Commonweal,* LXXXIII (October 1965), pp. 95–98.

Ignazio Silone and the Pseudonyms of God

> I could easily spin out my existence writing and rewriting
> the same story in the hope that I might end
> up understanding it and making it clear to others;
> just as in the Middle Ages there were monks whose
> entire lives were devoted to painting the face of
> Christ over and over again.
> —preface to the revised version
of Fontamara.

A first reading of Silone might give the impression that he is "dated." He is clearly writing about the struggle of Italian peasants against fascism in the 1930's, and about the lure of communism during that period as a possible alternative to the status quo. It could be argued that his works are no more than an interesting series of canvases depicting what life was like in a period and geographical setting now remote from us.

But to whatever degree Silone's main works were hammered out on the anvil of concern for the downtrodden and oppressed, and to whatever extent they rose out of particular challenges presented by fascism and communism, their author

20 has rightly seen that the story of the human spirit, threatened but not overcome during that period, is the story of the human spirit threatened but not overcome during every period.

Although the novels as originally written could stand on their own even today, Silone has employed the unusual device of rewriting a number of them, excising the materials that tie them too closely to the period of their origin, in order that the perennial concerns with which they deal may stand out in bolder relief. This he has done so far with *Fontamara* (1934, 1960), *Bread and Wine* (1937, 1962), *The School for Dictators* (1938, 1963), and *The Seed Beneath the Snow* (1942, 1965).

Whether the device is successful or even wise, the revised novels do force certain ongoing questions upon the reader, the events of the 1930's assume a disturbing relevance in the light of the events of the 1960's, and each one becomes a parable of contemporary human concerns. The parallels between the Italian "liberation" of Ethiopia and the American "liberation" of Vietnam are disturbing; the indictment of the indifference of the Italian church in the 1930's becomes an indictment of the indifference of the American church in the 1960's; and the disillusionment of the revolutionary in Silone's novels may foreshadow some of the problems with which the New Left must shortly come to grips.

The story Silone tells is, as he says, "the same story"—a story that needs retelling for each generation and in terms understandable to each generation. It is a story that is often told without explicit reference to the three-letter word g-o-d, but it is a story that is always grappling with what that word has meant for men, and with what the reality to which it is dimly pointing still means for men. Silone, deeply steeped in a Christian faith he has formally or at least institutionally rejected, finds it imposible to deal with that which has spoken most deeply to the human spirit without employing the imagery of Christian faith and Christian history. It is hard for one of sensitive conscience to affirm God's presence in the kind of world Silone depicts, so gross are the inequities between men, so brutal is the destruction of human values by nature using impersonal power and men using power impersonally. And yet, if God is absent, His absence is a kind of creative one, and is indeed almost a brooding presence, the presence of a God virtually at the mercy of His world; a God who, if He has visited His tortured planet, has gone into hiding; a God who, when He wishes to assert Himself must employ pseudonyms— false names—in order to communicate a healing word. That Silone has faith in a God not dead but hidden, a God found (when He is found) in the most unlikely places, is surely a central fact in that "same story" which Silone continues "writing and rewriting."

II

Dangerous though it is to use the events of an author's life as a means of understanding his works, the device is particularly helpful in the case of Silone, since his own pilgrimage is so close to that of many of the characters in his novels.

The terrible injustices of life around him were borne in upon Silone at an early age, as he recounts in an episode the reader might imagine to have come from one of his novels:

I was a child just five years old when, one Sunday, while crossing the little square of my native village with my mother leading me by the hand, I witnessed the cruel, stupid spectacle of one of the local gentry setting his great dog at a poor woman, a seamstress, who was just coming out of church. The wretched woman was flung to the ground, badly mauled, and her dress was torn to ribbons. Indignation in the village was general, but silent. I have never understood how the poor woman ever got the uphappy idea of taking proceedings against the squire; but the only result was to add a mockery of justice to the harm already done. Although, I must repeat, everybody pitied her and many people helped her secretly, the unfortunate woman could not find a single witness prepared to give evidence before the magistrate, nor a lawyer to conduct the prosecution. On the other hand, the squire's supposedly Left-Wing lawyer turned up

22 punctually, and so did a number of bribed witnesses, who
    perjured themselves by giving a grotesque version of what had
    happened, and accusing the woman of having provoked the
    dog. The magistrate—a most worthy, honest person in private
    life—acquitted the squire and condemned the poor woman
    to pay the costs.[1]

It became clear to Silone that attempts to combat such gross
miscarriages of justice were not going to be effected through
ordinary political means, since the whole system was rigged
against the peasants. He describes the decision of the large
landowner, "the Prince," to run for public office:

> The Prince was deigning to solicit "his" families for their vote
> so that he could become their deputy in parliament. The agents
> of the estate, who were working for the Prince, talked in
> impeccably liberal phrases: "Naturally," said they, "naturally,
> no one will be forced to vote for the Prince, that's understood;
> in the same way that no one, naturally, can force the Prince
> to allow people who don't vote for him to work on his land. This
> is the period of real liberty for everybody; you're free, and
> so is the Prince."[2]

The church played no role in the struggle, except to condone
by its silence the activities of the landlords against the peasants. Its priests were indifferent to the peasants' fight for justice, and anxious to support the status quo. Silone recalls seeing
a puppet show in which the devil marionette asked the village
children where the child in the show was hiding. The children
instinctively lied to save the child from the devil.

> Our parish priest, a most worthy, cultured and pious person,
> was not altogether pleased. We had told a lie, he warned us with
> a worried look. We had told it for good ends, of course, but
> still it remained a lie. One must never tell lies. "Not even to the
> devil?" we asked in surprise. "A lie is always a sin," the priest
> replied. "Even to the magistrate?" asked one of the boys. The
> priest rebuked him severely. "I'm here to teach you Christian
> doctrine and not to talk nonsense. *What happens outside
> the church is no concern of mine.*"[3]

Faced by injustice and dismayed by the impotence he felt at the possibility of bringing about change through ordinary political means or through the church, Silone joined the Communist party. He was a member for many years. But disillusionment with the party came too, in terms described later in this essay by Uliva, the disillusioned revolutionary of *Bread and Wine.* For Silone, and for Uliva, communism was indeed (in the title of the symposium from which the above excerpts are taken) "the god that failed." An act of faith had been made, an allegiance had been manifested, a commitment had been offered, and the god to whom the faith, the allegiance, and the commitment were made turned out to be a false god, an idol, a human creation rather than a deity worth dying for.

Silone finally left the party. He did not become a cynic, however, and after his departure he could still give voice to a positive credo that had been won at the cost of many scars:

My faith in Socialism (to which I think I can say my entire
life bears testimony) has remained more alive than ever in me.
In its essence, it has gone back to what it was when I first revolted
against the old social order; a refusal to admit the existence of
destiny, an extension of the ethical impulse from the restricted
individual and family sphere to the whole domain of human
activity, a need for effective brotherhood, an affirmation of the
superiority of the human person over all the economic and social
mechanisms which oppress him. As the years have gone by,
there has been added to this an intuition of man's dignity and a
feeling of reverence for that which in man is always trying to
outdistance itself, and lies at the root of his eternal disquiet.[4]

III

Where is God in the tangle in which Silone's political concerns have involved him? Where, in the novels written out of this experience, can one look for the divine reality? How does God relate to Silone's "intuition of man's dignity," to his "feeling of reverence for that which in man is always trying to out-

24 distance itself," and to man's "eternal disquiet?" It will not do
to try to make an orthodox Christian out of Silone, but as we
shall see, he draws heavily on orthodox and Biblical imagery in
dealing with the brooding presence of the divine. A description
of five interrelated themes may help us to see how the "shapeless god" takes shape in Silone's writings.

1. One might initially expect that God would be found
within the institution that exists to give Him honor and praise,
and that the church might be the abode of His human dwelling.
But the church, if it once gave witness to a Master who came
not to be served but to serve, seemingly does so no more. So
there is in Silone's fiction *a strong critique of the church*. Don
Benedetto, a priest in *Bread and Wine* who has been removed
from his post because of his advanced ideas, suggests to a
colleague that the church should condemn Mussolini's war
against Ethiopia. Don Angelo, a conservative priest, recounts
the conversation to Don Paolo:

> I replied, "But can you imagine what would happen if
> the Church were openly to condemn the present war? What
> persecutions it would undergo? What material and moral damage
> would be done?" You have no idea what Don Benedetto dared
> to answer me. "My dear Don Angelo," he answered, "can you
> imagine John the Baptist offering a concordat to Herod to
> escape decapitation? Can you imagine Jesus offering a concordat
> to Pontius Pilate to avoid being crucified?"
> "That doesn't seem to me to be an anti-Christian answer,"
> said Don Paolo.
> "But the Church is not a society in the abstract," said Don
> Angelo, raising his voice. "It is what it is. It's almost two thousand
> years old. It's not like a little girl who can permit herself all
> kinds of headstrong caprices. It's like an old, a very old lady,
> full of dignity, prestige, traditions, and rights tied to duties. Of
> course there was Jesus Who was crucified and Who founded her;
> but after Him there were the apostles and generations upon
> generations of saints and popes. The Church is no longer a
> clandestine sect in the catacombs. It has millions and millions
> of souls in its following who need her protection."[5]

But it is not only the far-off war against Ethiopia that the church will not condemn. There is another war nearer at hand, the war against injustice and poverty, with which the church refuses to involve itself. The story of this futile war is told poignantly in *Fontamara*, Silone's earliest novel. The peasants are tricked out of their water rights. The workers are tricked out of their pay by hidden taxes that become visible too late. When a movement of protest is finally launched, the town is pillaged, the women are raped, and finally the whole of Fontamara is destroyed. The book ends with the despairing cry:

What can we do?
After so much suffering, so many tears, and so many wounds,
so much hate, injustice, and desperation—
                    WHAT CAN WE DO?[6]

What they can do is what the narrators of *Fontamara* did— they can join the revolutionary forces.

What they cannot do is look to the church for help. The indictment of the church for its silence is epitomized by the dream of Zompa early in the book. The Pope and the Crucifix have a little talk. The Crucifix suggests all sorts of things the Pope could do for the people: the land could be given to the people, for example. The Pope counters that the Prince wouldn't have it, and the Prince is a good Christian. Christ then suggests that the peasants could be exonerated from their taxes; the Pope replies that the government officials couldn't think of that, and they are good Christians too. In response to the suggestion that the peasants be sent a good crop, the Pope replies that if there is a good crop, prices will go down and the merchants will be ruined; and the merchants are likewise good Christians. Finally Christ and the Pope visit the villages, with Christ carrying a knapsack from which the Pope can take anything that will do the peasants some good:

The two Heavenly Travelers saw the same thing in every village, and what else could they see? The peasants were lamenting, swearing, fighting, not knowing what to wear nor

26   what to eat. So the Pope felt his heart breaking, and he took from the sack a cloud of lice of a new species and sent them to the houses of the poor, saying, "Take them, O my beloved children, and scratch. Thus in your moments of temporal hate there will be something to take your thoughts away from sin."[7]

In *Bread and Wine* another priest, Don Piccirelli, writes a paper on "The Scourge of Our Times." Don Benedetto asks him hopefully, "Have you written about war or unemployment?"

"Those are political questions," answered Don Piccirelli stiffly. "In the diocesan bulletin we deal only with religious questions. From a purely spiritual point of view, the scourge of our times, in my opinion, is an immodest way of dressing."[8]

So much for the church's contribution to the social ills of men. It is no wonder that Rocco, in *A Handful of Blackberries*, gets up one day in the middle of mass and leaves the church, never to return. He suddenly realizes that those present are neither hot nor cold, and that God will spew them out of his mouth. Rocco chooses the poor as his comrades and makes his way into the Communist party, so that he can work for the social justice he has found the church ignoring. If God is a God who cares for those whom He has created, it is clear that the institution perpetuating His name has desecrated that name beyond redemption.

2. Where, then, is God found? Perhaps the God who appears to have been deserted by his church may be working in hidden fashion elsewhere. This possibility brings us to the heart of Silone's theme, his conviction that *God carries on His work through pseudonyms.*

Don Benedetto, the elderly priest in *Bread and Wine*, makes the point most directly: "In times of conspiratorial and secret struggle, the Lord is obliged to hide Himself and assume pseudonyms. Besides, and you know it, He does not attach very much importance to His name. . . . Might not the ideal of so-

cial justice that animates the masses today be one of the pseudonyms the Lord is using to free Himself from the control of the
churches and the banks?"[9]

Lest this seem too new an idea, too unorthodox in its implications, Don Benedetto makes clear in a conversation with his
former student Spina, now a revolutionary, that it has a long
history:

> This would not be the first time that the Eternal Father felt
> obligated to hide Himself and take a pseudonym. As you know,
> He has never taken the first name and the last name men have
> fastened on Him very seriously; quite to the contrary, He has
> warned men not to name Him in vain as His first commandment.
> And then, the Scriptures are full of clandestine life. Have you
> ever considered the real meaning of the flight into Egypt? And
> later, when he was an adult, was not Jesus forced several times
> to hide Himself and flee from the Judaeans?[10]

Don Benedetto also recalls the story of Elijah's encounter
with God (1 Kings 19:9–13). God was not present in the wind
or the earthquake or the fire—the accustomed signs of divine
theophany in those times. He was present, unexpectedly, in a
sound of soft stillness. So too today, he may not be present in
the open and public ways men expect him, but may be found
in quiet, hidden, unexpected deeds, in the pseudonymous activity of humble men. Reflecting on the Elijah story, Don Benedetto continues, describing certain actions in which he knows
Spina to have been involved:

> I, too, in the dregs of my afflictions, have asked myself:
> where is God and why has He abandoned us? Certainly the
> loudspeakers and bells announcing the new slaughter were not
> God. Nor were the cannon shots and the bombing of the
> Ethiopian villages, of which we read every day in the newspapers.
> But if one poor man gets up in the middle of the night and
> writes on the walls of the village with a piece of charcoal or
> varnish, "Down with the War," the presence of God is
> undoubtedly behind that man. How can one not recognize the

28   divine light in his scorn of danger and in his love for the so-called
enemies? Thus, if some simple workmen are condemned for
these reasons by a special tribunal, there's no need to hesitate to
know where God stands.[11]

The unexpectedness of the divine activity, the fact that God
may choose to work through pseudonyms is, as Don Benedetto
acknowledges, a familiar theme in Jewish and Christian history. The prophet Isaiah warned that in an ensuing battle between Israel and the Assyrians, the power of the Lord would
be revealed, but he made clear that the revelation would come
not through the chosen people of Israel but through the pagans
of Assyria. Assyria would be the "rod of God's anger," even
though the king of Assyria had no idea he was being so used,
and would have scoffed at the very notion.[12] Paul Tillich often
talks in similar fashion of "the latent church," the unexpected
instrument through which the divine may manifest itself, and
which may be quite different from the institutional church.[13]
Pascal similarly puts great store by Isaiah's discussion of the
hidden God: "Truly, thou art a God who hidest thyself."[14] God
can raise up children of Abraham from the very stones around
him. Since the churches do not serve Him, it may be that the
revolutionary forces can, and Don Benedetto later says of
Spina, "Socialism is his way of serving God."[15]

At different periods of history, God may employ different
pseudonyms. During the particular period about which Silone
is writing, when the grossest denial of God is the inequity between rich and poor, it can be expected that the manifestations
of God's presence will be found not among the rich, not among
the landlords, not among the heads of state, but among the
peasants. It is therefore highly consistent that the Christ figures in Silone's novels are drawn from among the peasants
(Berardo and Murica) or those who identify with the peasants
(Spina). The theme is present in *Fontamara*. Berardo, one of
the peasants who participates in the abortive uprising against
the landlords, is taken to jail, where he gets to know "the Solitary Stranger," the man seeking to organize the peasants. Re-

alizing how important it is for the Solitary Stranger to be at liberty, Berardo confesses to the crimes of which the Solitary Stranger has been charged, in order that the latter may be released. Berardo feels his own life can have a meaning if he dies not for himself but for someone else, and for a cause greater than himself. After Berardo's confession the authorities beat him up, and "finally they led him back to the cell, holding him by the arms and legs, like Christ when he was taken off the Cross."[16]

Berardo lays down his life for his friends, and his action finally galvanizes the peasants into action; they form a newspaper to give voice to their opposition to the landowners. They are crushed, as we have seen earlier, for victory is not yet something that is promised by God to men—a theme to which we shall presently return.

3. Silone, after his espousal of the revolutionary cause, does not become uncritical in that espousal. God may indeed choose to work pseudonymously through the forces of revolution, and socialism may indeed be a way of serving God, but Silone sees clearly that *the revolutionary forces, like the church, may also become corrupted.* When they do, they deny the God they unknowingly have served. The disillusionment of the revolutionary in several of Silone's novels mirrors the disillusionment that emerged from his own years as a communist. In *Bread and Wine*, Uliva, the disillusioned revolutionary, shocks Spina by the forcefulness of his attack upon that in which he once believed. Speaking about what will happen after the revolution, he says,

> Yes, I don't deny that there'll be technical and economic changes. Just as we now have the state railways and the state quinine, salt, matches and tobacco, so then we'll have state bread, state peas and potatoes. Will that be technical progress? Let's admit that it would be. But this technical progress will be an opening wedge for a compulsory official doctrine, for a totalitarian orthodoxy which will use all means, from movies to terrorism, to stamp out any heresy and tyrannize individual

30 thought. The present black inquisition will be followed by a
red inquisition. There'll be red censorship instead of the present
one, and red deportations will take the place of the ones we have
now—and the most favored victims will be dissident
revolutionaries. In the same way, just as the present bureaucracy
identifies itself with the fatherland and exterminates every
opponent, denouncing him as a hireling of the foreigners, your
future bureaucracy will identify itself with labor and Socialism
and will persecute anyone who continues to think with his own
head, as a prized agent of the big landowners and the
industrialists. . . .

For a long time I've been bothered about this: why have all
revolutions, every single one of them, begun as movements of
liberation and ended as tyrannies? Why hasn't even one revolution
escaped from this?[17]

Shortly after this outburst Uliva demonstrates the existential reality of his disillusionment by blowing himself and his
wife—along with a considerable portion of their apartment
house—to bits.

The same theme is stressed in *A Handful of Blackberries*.
Rocco, who walked out of church one day and joined the Communist party, makes the discovery that "the Party of today is
not what it used to be. It was a party of the persecuted, now it
is a party of persecutors."[18] So Rocco has to leave the party as
well, and there remains for him only a life of lonely protest
against all forms of corruption, a life spent as part of a remnant able to do little but wait for a day of deliverance that has
not yet come.

What has gone wrong? Why has the revolutionary cause
fallen victim to the malady it was trying to correct? For what
reason does it become increasingly difficult for Silone to
identify God's pseudonyms with the forces of revolution?

Perhaps the clearest answer is that in his concern for revolution on behalf of man, man himself becomes dehumanized, and
must find his way back from impersonal ideology to a recovery
of humanity. The progression of attitudes in Spina, whom we

first meet as a revolutionary-in-hiding in *Bread and Wine*, is   *31*
most instructive. At first he is simply one who organizes
groups for resistance, rebellion, and, possibly, death. But as the
book progresses, his enforced hiding results in his beginning to
enter into human relationships, to recover a feeling for *persons*,
and to discover that these are more important than impersonal
ideologies. He learns that one can find more human solidarity
in shared humanity than in shared political convictions. Spina,
disguised as Don Paolo, finds a young peasant named Infante,
follows him home and starts giving him a political lecture. Infante gives him food. Spina's landlady finally locates him in
Infante's hut and urges him to return to the inn for dinner:

> "I'm not hungry," said Don Paolo. "Go back to the inn,
> because I still have some things to discuss with my friend here."
> "Discuss?" said Matalena. "But don't you realize that he's a
> deaf-mute and understands nothing but some signs?"
> There was the deaf-mute, seated on the threshold of his hut,
> next to the priest. Don Paolo looked him in the face and saw how
> his eyes slowly realized the misunderstanding he had caused.
> The priest said to the woman, "That's all right. Go back to the
> inn anyway. I'm not hungry."
> The two men stayed there on the threshold of the hut, and he
> who had the gift of speech was silent. Every once in a while
> they smiled at one another. . . . After a while Don Paolo got up,
> shook hands with the deaf-mute and said good night.[19]

This seemingly trivial episode has deep significance for
Spina. His concerns shift more and more from politics to human love. In the sequel to *Bread and Wine*, *The Seed Beneath
the Snow*, Spina finally moves out of his own house and into
the stall with the deaf-mute Infante. A remarkable bond is
established between them, as Spina recalls in a conversation
later:

> "Brotherhood was the first new word which Infante learned
> from me. He could already say *bread*, which he pronounced *brod*;

32 and I explained to him with gestures that, in a certain sense, two people who ate the same bread became *brod-ers*, brothers, or companions. So from *brod* for *bread* came brother. The next day, Infante gave some evidence of his intelligence and of his agreement with my way of feeling when he showed me some mice running over the straw in search of bread crumbs. He murmured in my ear, "*Brod-ers*." From then on, he began to offer a piece of bread to the donkey every day, so that he could be a brother too, as he certainly deserved to be. I would like to talk a lot about my time in the stall, Nonna, and whenever I do, I'm trying to explain to you something of the state of my soul. Because I came out of there, if not completely transformed, at least stripped naked. It seems to me that up to that time I was not really myself; that I had been playing a part like an actor in the theatre, preparing a role properly, and declaiming the required formulas. All our life seems a theatrical fiction to me now.[20]

For Spina, what goes on in the stable turns out to be far more important than would have seemed possible to the earlier revolutionary; it establishes a human relationship across seemingly impossible barriers. This kind of relationship becomes more important to Spina than anything else, and finally, at the end of the book, when Infante has killed his father, Spina takes responsibility for the deed, confesses to the crime he did not commit, and lays down his life for his friend.

In *The Secret of Luca*, Andrea Cipriani, a politician, returns to his native village to run for public office. He arrives just at the time that Luca, a simple peasant, is released from jail. Luca has spent a lifetime in jail for a crime he did not commit, and which the people of the village know he did not commit. They are frightened by his return even though he seems to have no vengeance in his heart against those who could have demonstrated his innocence in court and failed to do so. Cipriani determines that he must discover the "secret" of Luca. What would motivate a man to let his life be destroyed in this way? Cipriani's attention is deflected more and more from his politicking as he discovers in Luca a fierce and stubborn integrity that was willing to endure forty years of imprisonment to protect the honor of another individual.

There is a dimension of human understanding that politics does not reveal. This does not mean that politics becomes unimportant, but only that politics needs, visionary as it may sound, to be infused by love. Without this ingredient, the most dedicated revolutionary will fall into the trap Uliva so convincingly sketches. The need is one that Rocco, both disillusioned churchman and disillusioned revolutionary, comes to sense. Rocco revises Descartes' *Cogito ergo sum* (I think, therefore I am) to *Amo ergo sum* (I love, therefore I am). This, it will be noted, is very different from the formula of another famous revolutionary, Albert Camus, who declared, "I rebel, therefore we are." Perhaps the fullest statement of the principle would even go beyond Rocco, and emerge as *Amo ergo sumus* (I love, therefore we are), since love must leap the boundary from the self to other selves.

Silone thus captures the disillusionment into which the revolutionary can be led, and he recognizes the ingredient that must enter into the ethos of the revolutionary if he is to avoid being transmuted into a replica of that which he wishes to overcome. That ingredient is love.

4. Once again, however, Silone does not fall victim of simplistic thinking. He offers no assurance that love will "win" or pay off. The one who loves does so at tremendous risk. And here again the theme of the pseudonyms of God comes to the forefront. For just as human love offers no assurance of success, neither does divine love. In his preface to *And He Did Hide Himself*, a stage version of *Bread and Wine*, Silone makes the point clearly: "In the sacred history of man on earth, it is still, alas, Good Friday. Men who "hunger and thirst after righteousness" are still derided, persecuted, put to death. The spirit of man is still forced to save itself in hiding."[21]

34   *"In the sacred history of man on earth, it is still, alas, Good Friday."* God has come to man, but man has not been willing to receive Him. Man has, in fact, rejected Him. God is present, not as triumphant presence, but as brooding presence, as suffering presence, a suffering into which those who "hunger and thirst after righteousness" can expect to be initiated. In his play, Silone introduces Brother Giocchino, a wandering friar, who has been expelled from his order for giving voice to the dangerous notion that Christ has not risen, that God is still in hiding, that it is still Good Friday. Brother Giocchino says to Uliva: "You have lost heart because you think [God] is here on earth no longer. But I say to you that He is still here on earth; in hiding, certainly, and in agony, but on this earth still. As long as He is not dead, we mustn't despair. And perhaps it is for us too see·that he is not allowed to die."[22]

The theme is not incidental to Silone, and he introduces it again in a later novel, *The Seed Beneath the Snow*. Don Marcantonio comments to a carpenter, Master Eutimio: "You forget that Jesus isn't on the cross any more. . . . The Church itself teaches that. There are people around here who believe that He's still on the cross, dying right now at this moment," said Master Eutimio seriously. "There are people who are convinced that He never died, and never ascended to heaven. That He's still dying, on this earth. And that would explain a lot."[23] The very symbolism of the book's title reinforces the point. The seed has indeed been planted, but it is still "the seed beneath the snow," the seed that has not yet come to flower. Furthermore, the action of the book takes place during Lent. Both facts suggest a theme of anticipation but not of fulfillment. The theme is reminiscent, as are so many of Silone's themes, of Pascal, who exclaims in the *Pensées*, "Jesus will be in agony even to the end of the world."[24]

That Christ has come to earth and has been crucified is, of course, part of the central Christian story. It is not the whole of that story, which includes the claim that Christ's death was not the end of the story, and that only in the light of His resurrection from the dead can ohe really bear the full burden of the message of the cross. There is, however, a Christian sentimentalism that leaps too quickly over Good Friday to Easter Sunday, that seeks victory without defeat and triumph without tragedy. It does not therefore understand the meaning of servanthood and suffering servanthood. In the face of such one-sided claims, Silone's counterclaim, that it is still Good Friday and that Easter has not come, is an important one. No victory worth having is ever cheaply won. Silone, however, refuses to let the unabated optimism of an Easter without Good Friday be transformed into the utter pessimism of a Good Friday without an Easter. For while he says that Easter has not come, he does not say that it cannot come. One can continue to hope, as Brother Giocchino does, and as all men must, but one must not allow his hope to be falsely and prematurely transformed into a nonexistent reality. There is a sober realism here that is clearly appropriated from the gospels, even though Silone himself is unable to make the full affirmation that the gospels make. While man must wait, he nevertheless waits with a certain hope, having seen in anticipation that which one day will be realized fully.

5. The above themes converge in a way that summarizes Silone's concern with God's pseudonyms. If God cannot be seen clearly and distinctly, if He is hidden by pseudonyms and it is still Good Friday, some hints of Him are nevertheless given to men. If He cannot be fully contained in human form or human events, there are at least certain events that help to reveal Him. *Earthly events can image divine events.* That which we experience in utterly human terms can contain portents of the hidden God.

We have already seen that the death of Berardo was more than the death of a peasant. It was a contemporary reenact-

36 ment of the death of Christ, a way of dramatizing the truth, "Greater love hath no man than this, that a man lay down his life for his friend."

In *And He Did Hide Himself*, Silone spells out in similar terms the implications of the death of another peasant, Luigi Murica. Murica had been found with a sheet of paper on which was written, "Truth and brotherhood shall triumph over lies and hatred," and "Living Labour shall triumph over money." Three women describe what followed:

THIRD WOMAN   Then they crowded round him, and put a chamber pot on his head for a crown, and in mockery they said to him: "This is the reign of Truth."

FIRST WOMAN   The wretches knew not what they did.

SECOND WOMAN   Then they put a broom in his right hand for a sceptre, and bowing to him they jeered: "This is the reign of brotherhood."

FIRST WOMAN   The wretches knew not what they did.

THIRD WOMAN   Then they took a red carpet from the floor and wrapped it round him in mimicry of royal purple.

FIRST WOMAN   The wretches knew not what they did.

SECOND WOMAN   Then they blindfolded him and lashed him to a pillar in the barracks yard.

FIRST WOMAN   The wretches knew not what they did.[25]

The conversation continues, paralleling the passion story.

Back in the village from which Murica had come, friends gather in his parents' home. They sit around the table. The elder Murica gives them food and drink, and the parallel to the holy eucharist, now being enacted in a simple peasant hut, is apparent.

"It was he," he said, "who helped to sow, to weed, to thresh, to mill grain from which this bread was made. Take it and eat it; this is his bread."

Some others arrived. The father gave them something to drink and said, "It was he who helped me to prune, to spray, to weed and to harvest the grapes which went into this wine. Drink; this is his wine."[26]

A little later in the meal, Spina comments, "The bread is made from many ears of grain. Therefore it signifies unity. The wine is made from many grapes, and therefore it, too, signifies unity. A unity of similar things, equal and united. Therefore it means truth and brotherhood, too; these are things which go well together." And an old man replies, "The bread and wine of communion. The grain and the grape which has been trampled upon. The body and the blood."[27]

The double meaning of this episode (from which the book's title is taken) is apparent. Bread and wine are necessities of life, imperative for sheer physical survival, and they thus stand for food and drink. But bread and wine stand for more than food and drink. Bread, as we have already seen, stands for companionship, for companions (*cum-panis*) are those who share their bread; and the bread and wine together, as Spina testifies, stand for unity, and thus for truth and brotherhood.

Silone, however, goes far beyond even such levels of meaning as these, for his account of the meal in the home of Luigi Murica's parents is shot through with allusions to the holy meal of Jesus and his disciples. The point surely is that it is not only the meal consumed at the altar in the church that is a holy meal, but that any meal, even in the rudest peasant's hut, can be a showing forth of the divine through the very vehicles of the earthy. Murica's body has been broken, and Murica's blood has been shed, on behalf of the victims of injustice, in the name of truth and brotherhood. And since he threshed the grain and trod the grapes, the bread and the wine are indeed "his" bread and "his" wine. But he who lays down his life for his friends witnesses not only to the integrity of his own deed, but witnesses also to the ongoing presence of the hidden God who has adopted the pseudonym of a suffering humanity.

In those moments when men suffer for their fellow men, therefore, they give shape to the "shapeless god" and make clear that God, too, participates in suffering on their behalf.

38   Silone makes apparent that the material can be the vehicle of the spiritual, and his very doing so destroys the propriety of such a way of speaking, for he is saying really that the material and the spiritual are indivisible, and that he who comprehends the one likewise comprehends the other. If it is unlikely that God should be present in a peasant's hut when eating and drinking are taking place, it is just as unlikely that He should be present in a Palestinian peasant's hut as the son of a village carpenter. He may be unexpected in either place, but His presence having been discerned in one place lends credence to His presence in other places as well. Every table can be holy, every meal a eucharist, every deed of love a revelation.

Silone's world is a world still unfinished. It has been confronted by the presence of God, and being unable to bear that presence has tried to destroy it. It has not succeeded in destroying that presence, although it has succeeded in forcing the divine into hiding, into the adoption of pseudonyms. But the divine continues to call upon men to discover Him in most unlikely places—in the man who writes in chalk "Down with the war," in the peasant who confesses to the crimes of another, in the revolutionary who teaches a deaf-mute the meaning of companionship—and thereby to assist Him in the work of bringing His own creation to completion. He is a strange, a hidden, a shapeless, a pseudonymous God, this God of Silone. But if men miss His presence in the world, it is not because He is not there, but simply because they have been looking for Him in the wrong places.

NOTES

1. Richard Crossman, ed., *The God That Failed* (New York, 1949), p. 83.
2. *Ibid.*, p. 86.
3. *Ibid.*, p. 85. Italics added. Silone later told the priest that if the devil marionette ever asked where the priest was, he would cheerfully give him the priest's address.
4. *Ibid.*, pp. 113–114.
5. Ignazio Silone, *Bread and Wine* (New York, 1962), p. 267.

6. Ignazio Silone, *Fontamara* (New York, 1961), p. 224.

7. *Ibid.*, p. 35.

8. *Bread and Wine*, p. 23.

9. *Bread and Wine* (earlier edition: New York, 1946), pp. 247–248

10. *Bread and Wine*, p. 274. The latter theme is developed in Silone's stage version of *Bread and Wine*, entitled *And He Did Hide Himself*, the Biblical reference being John 12:36: "These things spake Jesus and departed, and did hide himself from them."

11. *Ibid.*, pp. 275–276.

12. Cf. Isaiah 10:5–19.

13. Cf. most recently in *Systematic Theology*, III (Chicago: University of Chicago Press, 1963), esp. pp. 152–154.

14. Blaise Pascal, *Pensées*, Nos. 194, 242. The Scriptural reference is to Isaiah 45:15.

15. *Bread and Wine*, p. 305.

16. *Fontamara*, p. 211.

17. *Bread and Wine*, pp. 210–211.

18. Ignazio Silone, *A Handful of Blackberries* (New York, 1953), p. 145.

19. *Bread and Wine*, p. 148.

20. Ignazio Silone, *The Seed Beneath the Snow* (New York, 1965), pp. 194–195. The same point can be made linguistically from the Latin. *Cum-panis* means, "with bread," and it is the word from which "companion" is derived. Companions are those who share bread together.

21. Ignazio Silone, *And He Did Hide Himself* (London, 1946), p. 6.

22. *Ibid.*, pp. 62–63.

23. *The Seed Beneath the Snow*, p. 243.

24. *Pensées*, No. 552, "The Mystery of Jesus."

25. *And He Did Hide Himself*, pp. 102–103.

26. *Bread and Wine*, p. 322.

27. *Ibid.*, p. 323. The theme is present from earliest times in the second century document, the *Didache*, and is incorporated in most subsequent liturgies.

BIBLIOGRAPHICAL NOTE

Materials for the above essay are drawn chiefly from *Fontamara* (New York, 1960); *Bread and Wine* (New York, 1962); *And He Did Hide Himself* (London, 1946); *The Seed Beneath the Snow* (New York, 1965); *A Handful of Blackberries* (New York, 1953); and Silone's contribution to Richard Crossman, ed., *The God That Failed* (New York, 1949), pp. 76–115.

Other novels useful in the pursuit of these themes are *The Secret of*

40 *Luca* (London, 1962) and *The Fox and the Camellias* (New York, 1961). Silone has also written *Mr. Aristotle* (1955) and *The School for Dictators* (1938; 1963).

Useful secondary source materials are "Ignazio Silone: Novelist of the Revolutionary Sensibility," in Nathan Scott, *Rehearsals of Discomposure* (New York, 1952), pp. 66–111; "Ignazio Silone: The Politics of Charity," in R.W.B. Lewis, *The Picaresque Saint* (Philadelphia and New York, 1961), pp. 109–178; and "The Theme of the Remnant: Ignazio Silone's *A Handful of Blackberries*," in William R. Mueller, *The Prophetic Voice in Modern Fiction* (New York, 1959), pp. 158–183.

3 *A. A. DeVitis*

Religious Aspects in the
Novels of Graham Greene

Anyone approaching the work of Graham Greene is immediately confronted by a number of literary, scholarly, and, perhaps, theological problems; for Greene's career since the publication in 1929 of his first novel, *The Man Within*, has led him into many aspects of creative and imaginative literature. As well as his serious novels, he has written thrillers (which he calls "entertainments"), plays, motion picture scripts, essays, and several dozen short stories; more recently he has edited books for The Bodley Head Press. He has, besides, written countless reviews of novels and motion pictures for the *Spectator* and the *Times* but these enterprises date to his early career in the field of letters. In this category can be placed those pieces that appear from time to time in various magazines and journals from remote areas of the globe—from Indo-China, Cuba, and Haiti, places that frequently serve as locales for both his novels and his entertainments. Still, Greene is best known for his spy stories, such as *The Ministry of Fear* and *The Third Man*, and for his serious "novels," books that deal with "religious" problems.

According to many of his critics, Greene is a divided novelist who frequently doesn't know exactly where to place his em-

42 phasis—on action and suspense, as in the entertainments; or on characterization and philosophical speculation, as in the novels. To many of his readers, his religious, philosophical, and literary preoccupations range from Manicheism to latter-day Existentialism. Others see him simply as a writer whose Roman Catholicism is a device that allows him to comment on and perhaps even to play fast and loose with his one true love, the Church itself.

Perhaps there is a great deal of truth in this last assertion: the majority of his novels deal with people who happen to be Roman Catholics, people caught up in emotional dilemmas that give rise to theological speculations of the most beguiling kind. Frequently the solutions Greene implies for these very human problems do not seem consistent with the teachings of his church; and to that church he must stand as something of an enigma. But when one considers the general movement of Ecumenism, Greene's search for some sort of tolerance and understanding within the confines of his faith does not seem so very far from the new feeling the Catholic Church has been promulgating. The fact is that since his first novel Greene's career has involved him in an ever-widening circle of interests and beliefs that have taken him farther and farther from dogmatic Roman Catholicism toward a wider-ranging humanism; and it is this tendency towards humanism which places him strictly within the tradition of English letters, and marks at the same time his place as the most compelling and the best of modern novelists.

I

In 1938 appeared *Brighton Rock*, a novel that read much like a detective story, but one that upon reflection hardly seemed a detective story at all. In addition to the obvious paraphernalia of the thriller—the chase, the melodramatic contrivances, the sensational murders—that Greene had made use of in *The*

Ministry of Fear and *This Gun for Hire,* Greene presented an obvious allegory. The protagonist, an antihero named Pinkie Brown, was handled with a sophistication rare since Conrad, and the antagonist, a blowsy blonde named Ida Arnold, proved a bewildering as well as bewildered pursuer of the seventeen-year-old racketeer. That there must have been some confusion in Greene's mind about the kind of book he had written is apparent from his first calling *Brighton Rock* an "entertainment," and only later a "novel."

What is apparent now is that *Brighton Rock* was actually an attempt on Greene's part to explain the nature of right and wrong and good and evil in the world of ordinary men and women—good-hearted, generous, fine-feeling people like Ida Arnold. Still and all, people like Ida Arnold found themselves confused and bewildered when entering a world of good and evil, a world in which the values taught and insisted on were those of the Roman Catholic Church. Consequently, one of the most beguiling aspects of the novel is the subtle yet relentless way in which Greene managed to shift his reader's interest away from right and wrong—morally easy Ida—to good and evil—the Roman Catholic girl Rose and the boy Pinkie. As the focus shifted, the reader's affection for Ida diminished, and her undeniable humanity, at first so captivating, became tedious and then even unreal. The allegorical importunities of the theme began to dominate the narrative as the reader understood that Ida was merely a catalyst, the agent that precipitated a reaction that must have occurred in any event.

Within the allegory, Ida's concepts, right and wrong, are secondary to considerations of good and evil. Yet *Brighton Rock* is also a detective story, and within that pattern Ida Arnold exemplifies human nature and human justice—she is like a stick of Brighton rock candy: wherever one bites into it, it spells "Brighton." Ida is, however, an alien in the spiritual drama; she likens herself to a traveler in a foreign country who has neither phrase nor guidebook to help her find her way. She

44 is "a stickler where right's concerned," a competent pursuer of human justice, an avenging spirit, but an alien in a spiritual dilemma. She represents humanity; she is the vitality of most people, and the highest praise she can pay to any activity is that for her it is "fun." The reader sees her at first as friendly, good-natured, morally easy; but as the action progresses her "humanity" seems somehow to diminish as the reality of good and evil, a consideration Ida is not competent to understand, becomes infinitely more meaningful.

In turning to the girl Rose, the reader soon appreciates Greene's frightening comment made on Ida's world of right and wrong, this world of the everyday; for Rose is returned to the worst horror of all, a life without hope. On the recording that Pinkie had made for her she learns what her emotions have kept her incapable of appreciating—that Pinkie despised her and that her chief attraction to him had been her goodness, which he was determined to destroy. At the end of the novel Rose knows that she is pregnant with Pinkie's child; the reader is left to draw the conclusion that her marriage to Pinkie has been the union of heaven and hell. These, briefly noted, are the allegorical importunities of the theme; but the fact that the novel is also a detective story, and a brilliant one at that, should not be overlooked. *Brighton Rock* in 1938 begins for Greene a pattern of interest culminating with *The End of the Affair* in 1951. In the novels written between these dates Greene defines and clarifies his "religious" preoccupations without ever becoming a dogmatist or a religious teacher.

In an essay on the religious aspect of the writing of Henry James, included in *The Lost Childhood*, Greene writes, "The novelist depends preponderantly on his personal experience, the philosopher on correlating the experience of others, and the novelist's philosophy will always be a little lopsided." To this statement might be added a comment from *In Search of a Character* (1961): "I would claim not to be a writer of Catholic novels, but a novelist who in four or five books took characters

with Catholic ideas for his material. Nonetheless for years . . .
I found myself haunted by people who wanted help with
spiritual problems that I was incapable of giving." It would
seem then that the sensible approach to a study of the artistry
of Graham Greene is to take him at his own word. He is not
a "Catholic writer," considering the classification in its narrowest sense; he is not a novelist like G. K. Chesterton or
Helen White, who writes remarkably astute novels for Catholic girls. He is, as he says himself, a novelist who uses as his
characters people who happen to be Roman Catholics. The
sensible way to approach Greene's craft is to read what he
writes about his use of Roman Catholicism as background for
characters and plots in *Why Do I Write?*:

If I may be personal, I belong to a group, the Catholic Church,
which would present me with grave problems as a writer were
I not saved by my disloyalty. If my conscience were as acute as
M. Mauriac's showed itself to be in his essay *God and Mammon*,
I could not write a line. There are leaders of the Church who regard
literature as a means to an end, edification. I am not arguing that
literature is amoral, but that it presents a different moral, and
the personal morality of an individual is seldom identical with the
morality of the group to which he belongs. You remember the
black and white squares of Bishop Blougram's chess board. As a
novelist, I must be allowed to write from the point of view of the
black square as well as of the white: doubt and even denial must
be given their chance of self-expression, or how is one freer than
the Leningrad group?

The Power and the Glory (1940), grew out of a trip Greene
took through the Mexican provinces of Tabasco and Chiapas
in the late thirties. Here again Roman Catholicism is used as
background, and again it is allegory that lends the events of
the narrative an excitement above and beyond the simple
adventure of flight and pursuit. The whisky priest in the
Mexican novel is a reluctant recipient of grace, and to many
readers this fact immediately transforms the novel into a Cath-

46 olic document of such mysterious overtones that only the initiate can understand and appreciate it.

Greene's whisky priest is opposed by the lieutenant of the new order, the socialist state; neither protagonist nor antagonist is named, in keeping with the main theme of the novel, which is quite simply the portrayal of the meaning and value of the code handed down by Christianity since its inspiration by and in the New Testament. Yet in the final pages of the novel the priest becomes not so much a champion of Roman Catholicism or Christianity as a champion of the individual: in his dramatic debate with the lieutenant toward the end of the narrative he points out in his simple manner the real dignity of his humanity, something the lieutenant has been only reluctantly aware of.

The immediate frame of reference in *The Power and the Glory* is specifically the protagonist's Roman Catholicism, yet the ultimate referent is the humanistic ideal. The whisky priest is one who administers the sacraments of his church while in the state of mortal sin; he evades the police of the new state as he evades God, all the while sustaining his courage with drink. The theme of flight and pursuit is thus doubly pointed. In his characterization of the priest Greene consciously works within the anatomy of sainthood, a theme which was to preoccupy him in various ways until the publication of *The End of the Affair.*

In the Mexican novel Greene takes the weak priest who must drink to preserve his courage and through him portrays the thesis that the evil man discovers in himself is an index to his love of God. As a young man the unnamed priest had been good in the narrow and conventional sense. Concerned with sodalities and baptisms, he had been guilty of only venial sins; but he had felt love for no one except himself. Since the outlawing of Roman Catholicism in his province he has fallen to drink—and in a lonely hour fathered a child. It is his acquaintance with evil that allows him to learn about the resources of his religion. Closed in tight in a prison cell, aware with a precocious intensity of the foulness and stench of human misery, he recognizes the reality of evil and, conversely, feels the presence of God: "This place was very like the world; overcrowded with lust and crime and unhappy love; it stank to heaven; but he realized that after all it was possible to find peace there, when you knew for certain that the time was short."

In *Brighton Rock* Greene had sketched the theme of power in the relationship between Pinkie and his adopted father, Kite. In *The Power and the Glory* Greene develops his thesis in terms of the ironical similarities set up between the unnamed priest and lieutenant. It is through this representative of the new order that Greene portrays the vitality and strange beauty of power, subtly relating the cult of power to an ultimate consideration of evil. The battle of individual choice for good or evil is fought in the soul of the priest, who comes to represent individual protest against the degrading urges of power politics. In *The Lawless Roads* of 1939 Greene wrote: "Perhaps the only body in the world to-day which consistently—and sometimes successfully—opposes the totalitarian state is the Catholic Church."

The Power and the Glory, despite the fact that it apologizes in a very real way for the author's faith, nevertheless transcends its narrowly Roman Catholic theme. George Woodcock's observation in *The Writer and Politics* is in this respect cogent:

[W]hile the police lieutenant remains the representative of a collective idea, the servant of the State, the presence of the Church becomes steadily more distant and shadowy, and the priest seems to stand out more solidly as an individual, without tangible connections or allegiances, fighting a guerilla war for an idea which he considers right. Instead of being the representative of Catholicism, he becomes more and more the type of human person fighting against the unifying urges of a power society, and triumphing even in defeat and destruction, because in this battle

48   there are no fronts and the messages are passed on by examples to other individuals who continue as rebellious elements in the total State. This is an underground which is never eliminated, because it has no central committee and no headquarters, except in the heart of each man who feels the need for freedom.

As the whisky priest confronts the lieutenant and points out the evil of the organized violence he espouses, the Catholic Church fades more and more into the background; and as this happens the priest becomes more and more Everyman, seeking the ways and means to his own salvation and indicating at the same time the quality and nature of his convictions. In the character of the priest, Greene creates an important figure in contemporary mythology.

The Heart of the Matter, written in 1948, is the next major novel to develop and exploit religious considerations. Again there are allegorical importunities, but they are neither as obvious nor as insistent as they were in *Brighton Rock* and *The Power and the Glory*. In *The Heart of the Matter* the theme of pity, sketched in both the preceding novels, is given full expression by means of the central character, Major Scobie. Once again, this time in the careful characterization of the protagonist, the reader finds Greene working with myth: like the whisky priest Scobie escapes the immediate confines of the novel's situation and plot and becomes a character capable of exciting the curiosity, the imagination, and the humanity of the reader. The idea of Scobie remains with the reader long after he has forgotten about the intrigues of the melodramatic action.

Greene had successfully worked within the anatomy of pity in *The Ministry of Fear*, the entertainment that immediately preceded *The Heart of the Matter*; but the theme had not been distinctly related to a religious content. In both *The Ministry of Fear* and *The Heart of the Matter* pity is shown to be a force that dominates the personality and the actions of the protagonist, making him subject to the suffering of the world,

the victim of the unhappy and the discontented. This pity is
diagnosed as a sort of egotism, insisting as it does that the
individual assume responsibiltty for his fellow man without
consulting the referents of religion or philosophy. Hence pity
is shown to be an excess, and Greene comments indirectly on
the value of a religious or philosophical orientation that accounts for suffering. The aspect of pride can be neither overly
insisted upon nor ignored: Scobie's responsibility and concern
for unhappiness characterize him in such a way that he deludes himself, and perhaps the undiscriminating reader, into
thinking that he is essentially humble. And this is the paradox
upon which the characterization is built: Greene challenges
the reader to discover the error of Scobie's thought, while at
the same time he makes Scobie so human and so understandable that his error appears to be noble, as Prometheus's steal-
ing of fire from the gods appears noble to mankind. What
Greene achieves, then, is the creation of a man whose character flaw reaches tragic proportions.

The beguiling problem of whether or not Major Scobie is
saved according to the teachings of his Church has aroused
much speculation. Scobie's struggle with himself and with
his Roman Catholic God forms the basis of the conflict: it is
Scobie's pity that forces him to suicide. But to abstract from
the character's actions Greene's philosophy or personal belief
is absurd, for the novel has been constructed with an artistic
consideration in mind, not a philosophical or a religious one.
Both Arthur Rowe and Henry Scobie are moved by suffering,
misery, and ugliness. Unlike Rowe, whose preoccupation with
pity is put down to a childhood loss of innocence, Scobie is
possessed of a love of God that orients his actions and determines his suicide. The individual struggle is made the first consideration of the novel; as the character develops, the Roman
Catholic Church fades more and more into the background,
becoming a portion of the Necessity that propels Scobie on
his quest for identity and recognition.

50   As the action of the novel progresses, Scobie's pity and his sense of responsibility are described as images of his love of God. But Scobie's personal God is one of infinite mercy and forgiveness. As Scobie, a police officer in West Africa, goes off to investigate the suicide of a young district commander, he feels in his heart that his God will not exact damnation from one so young, so unformed. Father Clay, the district priest, attempts to reason with Scobie, but is interrupted: " 'Even the Church can't teach me that God doesn't pity the young . . .' " Scobie prefers the God who died for sinners over the God of justice and retribution; he chooses the God who allowed Himself to be crucified to prevent unhappiness over the God of justice. Scobie, then, trusts his own instincts concerning mercy and forgiveness above the written law. This is pride, but a pride compounded of a keen awareness and appreciation of unhappiness. For, paradoxically, it is his pride that makes Scobie humble; his intolerance of suffering is the index of his emotion. Indeed, the opposites seem irreconcilable, for Scobie accepts personally the responsibility for sin. But so had Christ. Scobie mistakenly sees himself in relation to Christ, who died to save mankind from the blight of the first sin.

Scobie is aware of this precarious logic, recognizing the possibility that the sense of pity he cherishes is an excess; but he knows equally well that he cannot avoid the call of misery and unhappiness. He reasons that with death, responsibility ends. " 'There's nothing more we can do about it,' " he says. " 'We can rest in peace.' "

Scobie's humility is evidenced by his willingness to accept the teachings of the Catholic Church for himself even though both his pride and his pity refuse to allow him to accept these same harsh strictures for others. He knows that if he kills himself to keep from hurting both his wife and his mistress (again he is mistaken, for his experience has shown him that no one person can arrange the happiness of another), he damns himself for all eternity. He does not so much fear hellfire as he does the permanent sense of loss of God that the Church teaches as a condition of hell. To be deprived of the God he loves is the worst torment of all for Scobie, yet he chooses this over giving more hurt to Louise and Helen. Sentimentally he sees himself as Christ committing suicide for mankind.

The Heart of the Matter takes its epigraph from Péguy: "The sinner is at the very heart of Christianity. No one is as competent as the sinner in matters of Christianity. No one, unless it is the saint." In *The Heart of the Matter* Scobie's competence in matters of his religion is shown all too clearly. His love, consistent with his pity, becomes indicative of a universal love. In the process of learning the substance of his religion he realizes the immensity of human love; he places himself alongside God and insists on dealing personally with matters of happiness. Both his pride and his humility, seen as opposite sides of the same coin, conspire against him. Paradoxically, since he refuses to trust the God he loves, he becomes at once Christ and Judas. He dies for man, but in doing so he betrays God.

Ultimately Scobie is a hero of tragic proportions. He knows his antagonist, recognizes his strength. What Scobie cannot accept is an orthodox conception of a God who seems indifferent to the agony of those He has created. He cannot conceive of a God who has not the same sense of pity as himself, and cannot trust a God who allows misery and unhappiness. Scobie is at once a scapegoat and a traitor, and his pity, mistaken though it may be in its applications, becomes his tragic flaw. Whether or not he is damned is unimportant in the consideration of his heroism or the novel's artistry. But Greene invites speculation and comment: the reader's concern for Scobie is, paradoxically, the most telling aspect of Greene's artistry; for Scobie's humanity is what most readers retain from the pages of the novel.

In *The End of the Affair* (1951) Greene creates a situation in which God becomes the lover of the heroine, Sarah Miles. At the expense of incident and action, the aspects of his art

52 which had stood him in best stead in the earlier pieces, he develops the theme that human love, even abandonment to passion, is an index to divine love.

Greene's narrative is set in the midst of contemporary events. Yet his minimizing the allegorical dimension and restricting the action of the novel to a bomb-torn city somehow detracts from the veracity of the presentation: the real world does not here appear as compelling as the symbolically conceived world of Brighton, Mexico, or West Africa.

Sarah Miles becomes a saint and Greene goes so far as to ascribe miracles to her. What the reader could have accepted in the earlier novels as compelling truth becomes in *The End of the Affair* embarrassing insistence on the author's part that his theme is significant and his method artistic. *The End of the Affair* is not completely successful because it is Catholic in the narrowest meaning of the term. *Brighton Rock* and *The Power and the Glory* had been Catholic in a broad sense and, ultimately, had escaped the limitations of Roman Catholicism because of the warm humanism upon which they insisted. However, Evelyn Waugh, who had severely criticized Greene's "theology" in *The Heart of the Matter*, applauded Greene's ability in using the religious theme in *The End of the Affair*, perhaps because he found the theological implications more acceptable within the framework of a Roman Catholic belief closely akin to his own orthodox views. "Mr. Greene is to be congratulated," wrote Waugh in the *Commonweal*, "on a fresh achievement. He shows that in middle life his mind is suppler and his interests wider than in youth. . . . He has triumphantly passed his climacteric where so many talents fail."

The action of *The End of the Affair* is limited chiefly to the ultimately unsuccessful love affair between Sarah Miles and Maurice Bendrix, an author who had not yet made the mistake of becoming popular. In *The Power and the Glory*, Greene had made use of "Bystanders," characters the whisky priest had encountered on his progress to martyrdom. The purpose of introducing these Bystanders into the action had been simply to indicate the force of Catholic action; in other words, to indicate that all the priest represents would continue in one way or another. In *The End of the Affair* Bystanders are made use of again; but here they emerge as important aspects of the plot, for it is their function to authenticate the various "miracles" attributed to Sarah after her death. They also add their perspectives to the story of Sarah, exemplifying various aspects of her character; yet they do not, somehow, succeed.

Paradoxically, *The End of the Affair*, although Greene's least successful novel among those discussed here, is his most artistically conceived and most "modern" novel, if one will except *The Comedians*, published in 1966. The melodramatic and allegorical contrivances, although the theme of flight and pursuit is still the chief pattern of the action, are replaced by the devices of "modern" fiction: the skeptical narrator, stream-of-consciousness technique, flashback, diary, interior reverie, spiritual debate, the found or discovered letter—all are used with discrimination and insight. Indeed, *The End of the Affair* is the most Jamesian of Greene's novels and also the one that most confirms in his work the influences of François Mauriac and Ford Madox Ford.

The function of Bendrix, Sarah's lover and the chief narrator of the novel, is to maintain a secular perspective on the events of the affair and to comment on the religious—here it might be more applicable to say Catholic—aspects of the theme. Like Charles Ryder in Evelyn Waugh's *Brideshead Revisited*, Bendrix is skeptical about what he calls the religious "hanky-panky" of the action, yet is the one left to make a final assessment of the meaning of the love affair. His last physical action is to begin writing the story of his and Sarah's relationship, and the implication is that perhaps he too, will learn to accept the reality of a divine force.

Bendrix's account of the affair dwells on its carnal side, its passionate side. Having established this point of view, Greene

54 allows Sarah's diary to fall into her jealous lover's hands; in this way Bendrix becomes aware of the spiritual struggle which is the basis of the novel. A third point of view is achieved by Parkis, an inept detective hired by Bendrix to spy on Sarah; a fourth by Sarah's husband Henry; and a fifth by Richard Smythe, a "rationalist" to whom Sarah goes in her need to deny the God who insists on her sanctity. But it is Bendrix who correlates and assesses these points of view. Here the reader finds himself in the same novelistic milieu that Ford Madox Ford so brilliantly describes in *The Good Soldier*, except that Bendrix's jealousy makes him infinitely more human than Dowell could ever be.

Sarah Miles's reluctant decision to prefer God over Bendrix is occasioned by her promise to give up Bendrix if God will allow him to live: she thinks he has been killed by a bomb that falls on the house where they have been making love. At first she tries to forget the promise, but she cannot. She suffers, as had Major Scobie before her, but her suffering teaches her to believe staunchly in the God who restored Bendrix. Her faith becomes her trust; and Greene insists that this trust is as firm as that which gave strength to the greatest saints. Sarah writes to Bendrix:

"I believe there's a God—I believe the whole bag of tricks; there's nothing I don't believe; they could subdivide the Trinity into a dozen parts and I'd believe. They could dig up records that Christ had been invented by Pilate to get himself promoted and I'd believe just the same. I've caught belief like a disease. I've fallen into belief like I fell in love."

The End of the Affair is technically Greene's masterpiece. The diary and the journal, the flashback, and the reverie all allow him not only to characterize his actors but also to present the various levels of Sarah and Bendrix's spiritual dilemmas. If *Brighton Rock* and *The Power and the Glory* owe something to Eliot's *The Waste Land*, then *The End of the Affair* owes as much to *Ash Wednesday*, for penance and acceptance con-

dition the atmosphere of the novel. If Major Scobie fails in
matters of trust, it is in these same matters of trust that Sarah
Miles triumphs.

II

Allegory and all the excitement occasioned by the contrivances of melodrama had given Greene ample latitude to
develop his themes in *Brighton Rock* and *The Power and the
Glory,* and, to some extent, in *The Heart of the Matter.* The
need to explain, clarify, and define had been a partial stimulus
for his writing these books. But in *The End of the Affair*
Greene discovered little need to allegorize, and melodrama
was kept to a minimum. The four novels indeed describe a
single pattern, a movement, from definition and qualification
of a religious conviction to a thumping avowal of the reality
of goodness in the real world. But one cannot forget that goodness had been present in the world of *Brighton Rock*: one
need only compare Rose to Sarah Miles to understand what
tremendous strides Greene made between 1938 and 1951 in
both characterization and novelistic technique.

Between the publication of *The End of the Affair* in 1951
and the appearance of *The Comedians* in 1966, Greene wrote
two major novels, *The Quiet American* in 1955, and *A Burnt-
Out Case* in 1961. Set in Indo-China, *The Quiet American*
exploits in terms of Conradian doubles the implications of
political innocence and philosophical experience. The English
journalist Fowler is paralleled by Alden Pyle, a naive American
intent on establishing contact with a mysterious power cult
headed by an equally mysterious General Thé. While paying
lip service to the tenets of contemporary Existential thought,
The Quiet American is in reality a further illustration of the
themes that interested Greene in *The Ministry of Fear* and
The Heart of the Matter: the fascination of power and its
destructive potential.

56 Pyle's political innocence is paralleled by Fowler's knowledge of the politics centering on the war-ravaged zone surrounding Vietnam and its neighboring countries. At the novel's end Fowler is forced to betray Pyle in order to keep the "innocent" American from contributing to the deaths of innocent people. Criticized by many American reviewers for its anti-American feeling, *The Quiet American* nevertheless makes a cogent point in a startling manner: what Greene intends, first, is to demonstrate satirically his belief that money cannot buy peace and security in a world coerced by power addicts; and, second, to insist that in a world on the brink of destruction, a man must choose to remain human, even if his choice imperils a personal equanimity dearly bought and paid for.

At the end of the novel Fowler says of the man he had betrayed to the Communists, " 'Am I the only one who really cared for Pyle?' " Although on the surface *The Quiet American* seems to exemplify the Existentialist formula of engagement and to give evidence of the *angoisse* necessary to a full appreciation of human involvement, the novel actually takes a sidewise glance at the theme of pity. Stripped of Major Scobie's sentimentality and high-sounding purpose, Fowler's reasons for betraying Pyle appear simply as egotism: the aspect of pity is perhaps replaced by that of compassion, much more difficult to appreciate. Fowler says, " 'I know myself and the depth of my selfishness. I cannot be at ease (and to be at ease is my chief wish) if someone is in pain. . . . Sometimes this is mistaken by the innocent for unselfishness, when all I am doing is sacrificing a small good . . . for the sake of a far greater good, a peace of mind, when I need think only of myself.' " Despite this assertion Fowler wishes after Pyle's death that there were someone to whom he could say he was sorry.

In the introduction to *A Burnt-Out Case*, Greene says that the task of writing the novel proved so difficult that he felt the

effort involved in writing still another to be beyond him. Indeed, there is something enervated about *A Burnt-Out Case*,
even though the craftsmanship of the novel is superb. The
Conradian elements emerge clearly and forcibly, even humor-
ously at times, but on the whole the novel remains unconvinc-
ing and the hero's plight unmoving. However, the ambience
of *The Comedians*, published in 1966, must have renewed
Greene's interest in the art of novel, and his effort was reward-
ed; it is one of the very best of his books and as exciting and
compelling as any of those written between 1929 and 1951.

The Comedians[1] is a black comedy, full of broad farcical
touches paralleled by frightening melodramatic innuendoes.
Perhaps the most significant aspect of the novel is that it gives
evidence of a shifting attitude on Greene's part toward his
Maker as well as toward his fellow man. *The Comedians* also
elaborates more fully on the theme of innocence, best exploited
previously in *The Quiet American*. There, Alden Pyle, thematically Fowler's alter ego, is the committed man; once in-
vestigated, however, the nature of his commitment is found
wanting. Through Pyle Greene attempts to indicate that innocence uninformed by experience is dangerous in a world
menaced by power cults. In *The Quiet American* Fowler is
forced to sacrifice Pyle to the cause of what he hopes to be
higher humanity, although he is by no means certain of his
personal motivations. What Fowler does know, and know for
certain, is that he cannot resist the appeal of the bodies
mangled by the explosion of Pyle's plastic bombs. In *A Burnt-
Out Case* the architect Querry makes his voyage into the
heart of Africa to rediscover the springs of innocence. Led by
Deo Gratias, a mutilated leper, to the very borders of innocence, Pendelé, Querry comes near to rediscovering the goodness he lost years before.

The hero, or rather antihero (for such he is), of *The
Comedians* is a man simply named Brown. (There are also
characters within the plot called Smith and Jones: the point,

58 perhaps, is to lend an Everyman aspect to the narrative.) With Brown, Greene attempts to define further the nature of innocence and that experience which is its opposite. In Greene's world, power is one of the many disguises of evil, and in *The Comedians* the fear engendered by power becomes the device by which the question of innocence is forced into prominence. The fact of the matter is that Greene in his last three novels has moved away from the highly stylized and symbolical representations—representations first employed in *Brighton Rock* and set aside after *The End of the Affair*—and has entered a new dimension, the outlines of which can only now be perceived.

Greene entitles his latest book *The Comedians*, and in the course of the novel's activity attempts to define what he means by the word "comedians," which, in turn, requires his establishing a definition of comedy. " 'Neither of us would ever die for love,' " says Brown to his mistress, Martha. " 'We would grieve and separate and find another. We belong to the world of comedy and not of tragedy.' " If *The Comedians* is a comedy, it is certainly not one in the accepted meaning of the term, nor in the Dantean sense; rather, it is Greene's version of contemporary black humor: there is no movement from despair to happiness—there is movement only from horror to despair.

The comedians are the pretenders, those who play a part, those neither good enough nor grand enough for tragedy—perhaps because Greene's world no longer allows for tragic action. Martha's husband, the ambassador of a small, unnamed South American country, says, " 'Come on, cheer up . . . let us all be comedians together . . . it's an honorable profession. If we could be good ones the world might gain at least a sense of style.' " But it is difficult to recognize the comedians, for frequently those who appear to be best qualified to play a part reach a point at which the part overwhelms them—the reality and the drama coalesce, or, to borrow Yeats's phrase, the dancer becomes indistinguishable from the dance. Occasionally one who assumes a role becomes the character he portrays, yet ironically the face he presents to the world continues to reveal eccentricity and grotesqueness. The comedians are nevertheless the worthwhile. They form a small troupe of initiates in a power-coerced and fear-ridden world. Still, it would be wrong to call tragedians those who manage to transcend the limitations of the role they play, for Greene's world, having once accommodated tragic action, no longer does so: at the novel's end the Haitian patriots are found symbolically housed in an abandoned insane asylum in Santo Domingo.

This question of innocence is at once the crux of and the key to the novels and the entertainments (*Our Man in Havana* appeared in 1958) published since Greene left off working with the anatomy of sainthood in *The End of the Affair*. In Sarah Miles, the strongest of his women characters, Greene carries the theme he had first presented in *Brighton Rock* to a final and disquieting conclusion—the impossibility of recognizing sainthood in a world hostile to saints, a world seemingly dedicated to the destruction of goodness. The recently published story, "Beneath the Garden," included in the collection significantly entitled *A Sense of Reality* (1963), is a further illustration of Greene's renewed interest in the anatomy of innocence, for that story is an expressionistic, occasionally absurd, and frequently humorous attempt to rediscover the point at which innocence was lost, to be replaced by the cynicism of experience.

The setting of *The Comedians* is contemporary Haiti under the dictatorship of Dr. Duvalier, "Papa Doc." Greene writes:

Poor Haiti itself and the character of Doctor Duvalier's rule are not invented, the latter not even blackened for dramatic effect. Impossible to deepen the night. The Tontons Macoute are full of men more evil than Concasseur; the interrupted funeral is drawn from fact; many a Joseph limps the streets of Port-au-Prince after his spell of torture, and, though I have never met the young Philipot, I have met guerrillas as courageous and as ill-trained in that former lunatic asylum near Santo Domingo. Only in Santo Domingo have things changed since I began this book—for the worse.

60 Like a Kafka enigma, Papa Doc remains mysteriously within his palace, his laws enforced by the Tontons Macoute, bogeymen, whose insignia are slouched hats and sunglasses, behind which they hide their uncertainties. The Voodoo element comes into play in the course of the novel's action, and an equation is drawn between Papa Doc and Baron Samedi, the prince of the dead of Voodoo belief. The Tontons approximate a mysterious fraternity of terror infinitely more menacing than that of the cultists. The chief representative of the power cult in the novel is Captain Concasseur, who is responsible for the mutilation and emasculation of Joseph, Brown's servant in the hotel Trianon.

Brown, Smith, and Jones arrive in Port-au-Prince on a Dutch vessel ominously called the *Medea*, Brown to return to his luxury hotel which he has been unsuccessfully trying to sell in the United States; Smith, a former presidential candidate who ran against Truman on a vegetarian ticket in 1948, together with his wife, to set up a vegetarian center; and Jones, an inept adventurer who calls himself "Major," to engage in a military maneuver of dubious nature.

Brown has been conducting a love affair with Martha Pineda, the wife of a South American diplomat. She is the mother of a five-year-old child, Angel, whose claims keep her from abandoning her family for Brown, whom she says she loves. The affair, bittersweet and reminiscent of many love triangles in Greene's fiction, is resumed the night Brown returns to Haiti. Brown admits several times that what he seeks in a love affair is not so much happiness as defeat; and ironically there is a sort of success at the novel's end—Brown and Martha both realize once they are safely over the border in Santo Domingo that their love affair belongs peculiarly to Port-au-Prince, that it was but the reflection of the horror and terror of the times.

Brown has been brought up a Catholic, but he is unlike the Catholics Greene has previously portrayed. The passionate pity of both Scobie and Fowler has given way to a tragicomic compassion, which is also the chief mood of the novel; Brown is much more tolerant of success than any of Greene's other heroes, but he is infinitely less loving. His Catholicism is not the leper's bell that it is to both the whisky priest and Sarah Miles; it is instead a cloak of indifference, a means whereby the stupidities and the atrocities of the world can be warded off, and perhaps explained. Brown's Catholicism becomes for him a standard of measurement, in Haiti a valid one, for Catholicism liberally sprinkled with Voodooism is the religion of the majority.

Through the Smiths, or perhaps because of the Smiths, Greene expresses a certain amount of anti-American sentiment reminiscent of *The Quiet American.* Dr. Magiot remarks at one point:

We are an evil scum floating a few miles from Florida, and no American will help us with arms or money or counsel. We learned a few years back what their counsel meant. There was a resistance group here who were in touch with a sympathizer in the American embassy: they were promised all kinds of moral support, but the information went straight back to the C.I.A. by a very direct route to Papa Doc. You can imagine what happened to the group. The state department didn't want any disturbance in the Caribbean.

Although he bears much in common with Alden Pyle of *The Quiet American,* the good vegetarian Mr. Smith is by no means the same sort of deluded innocent. He is capable of appreciating the opportunism and graft-seeking of the corrupt Tontons Macoute; and he even has the courage to admit that his vision of setting up an American Vegetarian Center in either Port-au-Prince or the new city, Duvalierville, is impractical. Despite their being vehicles for caustic satire, Mr. and Mrs. Smith emerge as the two strongest characters in the novel; they are saved by their humanity, by their certainty that there is goodness in the world. Ultimately, it is their dedication to their cause, their sincere and straightforward desire to better the

62 human predicament—by reducing acidity in the human body —that makes them acceptable.

It is also through the Smiths that the theme of commitment enters the novel, again satirically. As in *The Quiet American*, Existentialism is used as a philosophical determinant, but in this novel it is not so much obscured by religious considerations. Furthermore, the jargon of Existentialism is kept to a minimum and the theme emerges more cogently, demonstrated as it is in the action of the comedians who make up the drama.

"Major" Jones, who at first appears to be the biggest fraud of all, one of the "tarts," as he puts it, is a committed man by the novel's end; but his commitment is comically handled. He passes himself off as an organizer of military affairs, but he fools only those who wish to be fooled. He dreams, he invents, and he deludes, at times even himself. But there is something about the man that endears him to others. Tin Tin, the girl at Mère Catherine's bordello, likes him because he makes her laugh; and Brown's mistress Martha, in whose embassy Jones takes shelter when his bogus papers are discovered by Captain Concasseur, likes him too, and for the same reason—he makes her laugh. Brown, we are told, has never learned the trick of laughter.

Together with Dr. Magiot, a committed Communist, Brown arranges for Jones to escape the Tontons and to join the partisans, who under Philipot, a one-time Baudelairean poet, are attempting to unseat Papa Doc in bumbling and ineffectual ways. However, Brown's decision to help the partisans is motivated not by a feeling for the rightness of their cause, or by the danger and the excitement, or by his awareness of the child-like innocence of their exploit, but by the unreasoning jealousy that he feels toward Jones. Again, the reader is reminded of Fowler. Jones is a comedian within the broadest meaning of the term; but unlike Brown who cannot—perhaps because of early Roman Catholic training—he can follow the gleam, and there comes a point where the dream and reality coalesce. In his last glimpse of Jones, the reader sees him limping along, unable to keep up with the partisans because of his flat feet. He remains behind, a comical version of Hemingway's Robert Jordan, to fire upon the Tontons in order to make it possible for those he has grown to love to survive, if only temporarily.

Of all the major comedians, Brown alone remains uncommitted. He is a con man grown old, whose most successful venture had been peddling bad pictuures to the nouveaux riches. His mother's postcard had brought him to the Trianon, and one of her first questions had been, " 'What part are you playing now?' " After her death, Brown had discovered among her papers a note she had written to her young lover: " 'Marcel, I know I'm an old woman and as you say a bit of an actress. But please go on pretending. As long as we pretend we escape. Pretend that I love you like a mistress. Pretend that you love me like a lover. Pretend that I would die for you and that you would die for me.' " Brown's love affair with Martha, however, is something more than just pretending; it is a desperate attempt to capture stability in a fear-menaced world, and it is compounded as much of the desire to inflict pain as it is of a desire to dominate. For several years Brown has prospered, achieving a false sense of security; but the coming of Papa Doc and the Tontons has destroyed not only his business but his sense of belonging as well. He finds himself involved with innocence, with the Smiths and with Jones, who, thematically, serve to set off and to illustrate his failure.

The problem of Brown's Roman Catholicism is an important one in understanding both the characterization of Brown himself and the theme of the novel; it is indeed the chief challenge of the book. The Voodoo black mass in which Brown's servant Joseph participates makes a sensational counterpoint to the religious importunities of the novel; the figure of Baron Samedi is associated with Papa Doc, the personification of evil. But the black mass does not necessarily suggest a breakdown of religion. At the novel's end, it is contrasted with the mass the

64 priest reads over the body of Joseph in the insane asylum in Santo Domingo where the partisans are cared for. Brown's failure, then, does not illustrate a religious breakdown; it is a failure of character.

Brown's failure is his inability to accept reality, and it can best be explained in Existential terms. He can detect innocence, appreciate goodness, admire courage, and—even if for the wrong motives—help the cause of right. But he is so good a comedian that he cannot transcend the limitations imposed by the role. All the religious implications seem like so much rationalization on Brown's part, and he fools neither himself nor the reader. Brown can appreciate commitment: to retain his self-esteem, to support his ego, he is forced into comedy. Although his sympathies are with Dr. Magiot, Philipot, and the partisan cause, Brown makes no real commitment to anything, not to love, not to religion, not to God, not to innocence. It is only right that at the novel's end Brown becomes a partner in the undertaking business. In his black suit and black hat he appears a comic Baron Samedi. He belongs to the world of the dead and not to that of the living, and symbolically and literally he serves the dead.

Since the appearance of *The Man Within* critics have accused Greene of being pessimistic. The truth of the matter is that he is not a cheerful writer, but *The Comedians*, tragicomic though it is, and full of comic touches and humor of a macabre and grotesque nature, is the gloomiest of his novels to date. At least Major Scobie loves God, in his own mistaken way; at least the whisky priest finds honor, albeit unwillingly; and Sarah Miles achieves a sort of gratuitous sainthood. Querry in *A Burnt-Out Case* finds the hint of an explanation; he glimpses Pendelé. But there is only a pathetic part left for Brown to play in *The Comedians*. There is not even the saving factor of remorse as in *The Quiet American*; for Fowler wishes at the end of that novel that there were someone to whom he could say he is sorry for his participation in Pyle's death. Fowler at least

is spurred to action after witnessing the carnage caused by
Pyle's plastic explosives. He does what he does because he
loves. But there is no real love in Brown, only ego. Jones and
Smith may indeed illustrate contrasting aspects of the theme
of innocence, but within the pattern of the novel they serve
merely as foils to set off the failure of the individual.

NOTES

1. Portions of this section of the argument were published in
Renascence, Winter 1966.

4

Herbert Howarth

Quelling the Riot:
Evelyn Waugh's Progress

The critics who lit with pleasure at Evelyn Waugh's earliest novels anticipated a rake's progress; he gave them a pilgrim's. Their praises became a little rueful; and he listened without self-deception. Introducing a new edition of *A Handful of Dust* thirty years after its first appearance he remarked, "This book found favour with the critics who date my decline from it." Much as they admired the grim pages they mourned the extinction of the iconoclastic inventions and the quick, exhilarating prose of its predecessors:

> You grow correct, that once with Rapture writ,
> And are, besides, too *moral* for a Wit.

Decline and fall, indeed! But did Waugh's contemporaries see his work quite clearly? A year or two after his death it already looks different. This essay is an attempt to retrace his path, to understand certain conditions of his journey, and to honour the persistence with which, against recurrent problems, he stuck to his course.

In rebound from a war a society jettisons the values of the world which produced and permitted the holocaust. The twenties were years of rebound. In Germany they were years of

68 brilliant riot (creative but eventually disastrous). In England something less. The mood, says Ford Madox Ford, remembering the maroons which signalled the armistice of autumn, 1918, was "No more respect . . . For the Equator! For the Metric system! For Sir Walter Scott! Or George Washington! Or Abraham Lincoln! Or the Seventh Commandment!" It was a mere foretaste of the Berlin-rivalling England to ensue on the Second World War (brilliantly creative, in peril of disaster; to be saved, we hope, by a ballast of sanity). But a group of wealthy and titled fledglings, beaux and sylphs, in London, Oxford, and Cambridge, made a bid for a semblance, a lustrous fake, of anarchy. And in the arts there briefly flourished an attempt like theirs to thrive without an interior, to be rippling surface. Examples are the social-occasion stories with which Eliot and Vivienne Eliot experimented in the *Criterion*; the early novels of Aldous Huxley; and Evelyn Waugh's first two novels, which came at the end of the decade and only just in time before the masquing lost momentum and a new seriousness arrived.

Early Waugh is elegant as Pope, grotesque as Smollett, morning-brisk as Prokofiev. *Decline and Fall* is Waugh's *Rape of the Lock*: it mocks the follies of the crush, yet is bright with the privilege of participation. Liberated by the day's madness, the freebooter overplot sprints forward; is checked, in parody of the eighteenth-century novelists, by a fantastic narration, but this is rapid too; and sprints forward again. Dialogue and commentary are close-pruned. Recall the tale after twenty years, and you may think that Waugh indulges himself here and there: that he saunters *andantino grazioso* from Berkeley Square up Hay Hill to Dover Street. Refresh your memory from the text, and you find that the effect is accomplished with five direct sentences, four of them factual. Out of taut prose Waugh distils a lyric suggestion that life is gay—liable to abrupt punctuation, but gay.

In a book where fantasy runs free it is easy to find Waugh's "permanent images." Montaged over Paul's reflections in prison—his half-regret at taking the rap for Margot Beste-Chetwynde, his half-satisfaction—is Waugh's image of beauty. Margot is beautiful. Would Paul have wished to see her scrubbing in the prison-laundry for the sake of mere justice? "As he studied Margot's photograph . . . he was strengthened in the belief that there was, in fact, and should be, one law for her and another for himself, and that the raw little exertions of nineteenth-century Radicals were essentially base and trivial and misdirected." In 1928 this seemed a youthful caper, part of the anti-value riot, a squib under the throne of humanitarianism. It firmed into an attitude: beauty is a joy for ever; beauty must come first; all things broken and ugly and all people broken and ugly, must be swept out of the way. Preserve Marie Antoinette, and let the mob starve. I assume that we know all that can be felt and said against this. But we may respect the man who comes out fighting for it. Waugh fights for it:—against our humanitarian phalanx, and against an opposition he may dread more: the teaching of his Church. This is one of the problems of his journey.

The air of *Decline and Fall* is astringently sunlit. In *Vile Bodies*, for all the piquant episodes, there is a darkening: crepitation of storm, London fog, the coming war. Eliot, whose poems had seized Waugh at Oxford, whom he repeatedly quotes or echoes, and with whose path his journey crisscrosses, had said that under the sheen of the parties and ragtime lay a corrosive ennui. "*What a lot of parties,*" Waugh now says, ". . . all that succession and repetition of massed humanity. . . . Those vile bodies." The nausea and shadow are symptoms of an invading moral sense.

In 1930, three years after Eliot, harried by freedom, took sanctuary in the Anglican Church, Waugh was received into the Roman Catholic Church. In England the Roman was for three centuries an oppressed Church; and her English members still have the awareness of a minority, and the pride, to which they are entitled, of having borne and outstayed the years of

70   disadvantage. Waugh, by nature addicted, and by Oxford encouraged, to lonely causes and the joy of fighting against odds, yet conservative, and dismayed by fragmentation and chaos, found a double fulfilment in conversion: as a Roman Catholic he fused with a world-body and became concentric and at peace, and as an English Roman Catholic he appeared to family, friends, and to that public whom he regarded as the Mob and whose faces he hardly distinguished, as eccentric and militant.

    The next novel, *Black Mischief* of 1932, is a battleground between two Waughs: the man with a new Catholic life; another unregenerate Waugh, the fiercer for the submission of his counterpart. Not that the Catholic Waugh overtly presents his faith, in this extravaganza. There is only one momentary manifestation of the "neo-Catholic novel": a Canadian priest, muscular, red-bearded, cigar-smoking, straight-talking and "occupied in shaking almost to death the brigade sergeant-major of the Imperial Guard." He is a tentative towards the new image of the Roman priest, such as Ford Madox Ford had beautifully sketched in Father Consett in *Parade's End* and Graham Greene was to perfect in several variations (an image to erase and replace the fearsome image of Rome current among nineteenth-century English non-Catholics). The plot, however, is shaped to serve the faith. Barbaric Azania, void of loyalty, cannibalistic, is the type of the world without a Western Church. But movements from the deep drive against the flow of the story. Inmost Africa—which, like Gide and Malraux, like Greene and van der Post, he has gone exploring (let Eliot read Frazer at home and scent the ritual in Stravinsky's theatre, these have taken their anthropology on their own hides)—is an inmost part of Waugh. Penitent at Rome, Augustan at his desk, he yet sits in the drumming circle and dips into the cauldron, consumes the scrap of marrow and digests the victim's mana. Basil Seal, who comes into literature with this book, is an amphibian from the undertow of Waugh's psyche. A "corker" in good looks and masculine endowment, hard-drinker, brawler, manipulator of many languages, every etiquette, every know-how, Basil Seal is the continuation of the world-anarchy of the twenties and Waugh's personal anarchy: an aggressive, ruthless, refusal to conform which is at the core of his nature, and which lashes out of the depths in sudden farcical fury at his conscious obedience to a civilizing Church.

His truculent and wilful resistance to the norms of his day, and a special pleasure in offending the liberal and the humanitarian, find some outlet in almost every book. A phrase in *Black Mischief* will illustrate. Out of the hills, where, reversing the expectations into which the first chapter has decoyed us, he has won Seth's battle, and therefore at this moment a kind of hero, comes General Connolly. He was a stocky Irishman, says Waugh, and then tosses his curriculum at us: ". . . service in the Black and Tans. . . ." Name of obloquy! Approve it or not, Waugh seems to challenge, toughness makes a better man than *bonne volonté*. There is more than a touch of Kipling in the paragraph. Where everyone else has conspired to sell or desert Seth, the white General has stood fast. Waugh deliberately dons imperialism and other untimely codes, and wears them with defiance.

But with the writing of *Black Mischief* and the nightmare of *The Man who liked Dickens*, the protesting anarchists in him were for the while played out and placated. He turned to a moral work. *A Handful of Dust* is one of those searingly anaphrodisiac dramas to which Eliot's *Waste Land* gave rise (and the genealogy is the clearer for Waugh's title). It lists the whimsical and unnecessary steps by which Brenda Last gets into adultery, the absurdity of her interest in a clod, his predatory motives for getting in, and then for getting out, the spiralling of her passion till, at the apex of Waugh's predication (which is nothing but succinct reporting), she thanks God that her child is dead and not her lover. The terseness heightens the horror, suggests the concentrated strength of that disgust at vile bodies which stirred in the phrase of 1930. The bodies of 1934 are his friends of 1928 and 1930; they play their adulteries in the restaurants, parties, and flats where he formerly found amusement. There is no perfume in Metroland for the Waugh of this book.

Delight has moved to the country. Tony Last is "madly feudal." His roots—with all the organic vitality of that metaphor—are in his family home, Hetton. His thoughts and his money are devoted to maintaining it, to maintaining its servants and pensioners, to keeping it intact for the family in the future. From the aberrant Brenda he accepts every injury and imposition until he learns that she requires him to sell Hetton. Then the worm turns. Waugh has deployed his pieces, as a novelist traditionally may, so that the reader, up to this moment enraged by the accumulating successes of adultery, is elated that the adulterers get their come-uppance and is lifted on the wave of sentiment we call "wanting to cheer." But: *we* are glad that Tony Last defends *himself*; *Waugh* is glad that he defends the *house*. Waugh has adopted what will henceforward be a principal position: the great English house, which, if it is not now a Catholic house, must have been so in the past, is both the embodiment of beauty and the repository of tradition and faith.

As a social ideology, in fact as "Young England," feudal England has been the habitat of some good writers for a hundred and twenty five years since Disraeli by a sense of opportunity and an imaginative flare-up plied the reveries of Lord John Manners into *Coningsby* and *Sybil*. Against the avaricious competitive commercialism of his day, and the hard-heartedness of the Liberal creed of work, Manners dreamed of a stable non-competitive order: the classes graded, but the grades interdependent; and the higher a man's rank the more onerous his responsibilities to the ranks below. In his plan men would relate not to the distant capital city but to a great house, the manor of the mediaeval organization; and the lord or magnate must live constantly in his house, *visibly* fulfilling his duties to his district and radiating life from his central presence. This legend, this doctrine (it is more than the one and less than the other), burgeoned in minds well aware that the Middle Ages were sweetened by distance and Sir Walter Scott, but in love with the idea of reciprocal decency. It has intertwined, though not by any official cultivation, with the thought of the revived Roman Church in England. It is an important constituent of the neo-Catholic novel, present in the most refined practitioner, Ford Madox Ford, as in the most popular, G. K. Chesterton. When Waugh describes himself in the strenuously crusty opening pages of *Pinfold* as an idiosyncratic Tory, he is slightly mistaken. His Toryism is not idiosyncratic. He is one of the remarkable group descended from Young England. *A Handful of Dust* signals his allegiance. *Brideshead Revisited* and the war trilogy confirm it.

After predication, a nimble turn back to Africa and farce. With *Scoop* at their disposal, it is hard to decide why the critics accused, accuse, Waugh's comedy of dessication. *Scoop* is a spectacular lampoon on the Press and the politicians. It is grotesque in Waugh's Smollett vein, and is counterpoised in Smollett's way by Smollett's sort of insular sentiment. The protagonist, Boot of Boot Magna, is the sentimentalist's English country-gentleman: naive, unworldly, self-effacing, but, once roused by injustice, resolute in retaliation. Tapping out his famous cablegram to smash Dr. Benito and avenge Kätchen, Boot is a light-hearted version of Tony cutting up rough to save the feudal system.

Insular sentiment? Waugh is insular, again and again. It is a part of the reactionary pose (it accords well with the repertoire of attitudes struck by the marvellous father in *Work Suspended*). But just discernible is another Waugh with an extra-insular sensibility. Kätchen's story shows that, even before the forties, when everybody began to hear of statelessness, Waugh knew a little of the out-Europeans, who make their way

74 across the world with no passports but courage and wit. In Graham Greene's hands Kätchen and her prospector husband would have grown to figures of unforgettable pathos. But Greene's special art lies outside Waugh's range; and even if graced with the resources Waugh would not have disturbed the balance of his comedy. But he says just enough, as he works with quick strokes, to lay bare a nerve and infer another tale, a more acrid mood.

Work Suspended, the first two parts of a novel interrupted by the outbreak of war, has a keen beauty. He appears to have been working towards a full-length study of love. The pages in some respects anticipate *Brideshead*; but into *Brideshead*, when the time came to write it, different tones crept, for by then many bridges had been destroyed by war.

Waugh gave up his novel to enlist. Like Guy Crouchback he felt the satisfaction of the opportunity to strike back at "the Modern Age in arms"; and the Basil Seal, the "tough nut," in him saw the chance to emerge cloaked and daggered and live with royal licence the "exhilarating days" of which the dedication to *Officers and Gentlemen* speaks. Though he had suspended a good novel when the events of August 25, 1939, broke up an epoch, and though he could never revert to it, he formed new literary projects within a year. Physical work fertilizes a writer. His brother Alec found it easy to complete a novel during active soldiering in the First War, and easy again when he was with his regiment at the outset of the Second. Evelyn Waugh wrote throughout his service with the Marines and the Commandos.

Put Out More Flags, a sketch-book of England adapting to the struggle during the first year of sparring, is organized on Waugh's favourite binary plan. One object is to graph the first eddies of a new spirit in Britain. The playboys who were tarring Mercury or debagging Paul Pennyfeather, and running the dirigible party or reeling to the Old Hundredth, now one by one find their way to the Commandos. Qualities which had lain unelicited, or which Waugh had not been ready to notice, appear in them. Basil Seal comes to the help of Angela Lyne, drinks chivalrously with her to guard her from over-drinking alone. He marries her with an attractive non-avidity for her wealth. Beside the guts, which we always knew him to have, the appalling Seal discloses a fundamental stratum of decency. That is one tide of the novel. And the counter-tide? Boobyism. Waugh dramatizes the smugness, folly, and blobs of officialdom and its bevy of Sir Josephs. In the earlier books he has occasionally jeered, in *Vile Bodies* at the Premier benignly and the censorship-bent Home Secretary less benignly, in *Scoop* at the sale of titles. He and his friends probably regarded this spoofing as merely convivial. The spoofing of *Put Out More Flags* is, not more purposeful, for it is unlikely that Waugh expected his victims to be changed by it—in fact, the seriousness of the matter shows most in his cynicism, his doubts whether any change can be accomplished—but more deeply-felt: the nation may bumble along in peacetime, but in the emergency of war sanity should take over; whereas he sees insanity and complacency on the loose. To say so, with a fitting hyper-fantasy, is the job of a satirist

> So proud, I am no Slave:
> So impudent, I own myself no Knave:
> So odd, my Country's Ruin makes me grave.

In the tracks of Pope Waugh has graduated from pleasure to anger. An angry ridicule drives the counter-tide of *Put Out More Flags*; and it is renewed in the trilogy when Waugh looks back at the six years of military crisis and judges them as a whole.

In the middle of war he turns his gaze to the past, which looks lovelier for the contrast. Parting company now from the Eliot who declared the years of *l'entre deux guerres* largely wasted, he writes *Brideshead Revisited* to commemorate a period of delight; but also to justify its passing. He finishes his manuscript in a mood of authorial bliss. In Algiers he sits before Diana Duff Cooper, as if he were Basil sitting before Sonia, and tells her that he has written his masterpiece. It is evident, from the carefully-conventional similes stitched across the narrative, that he aimed at epic: the epic of the twenty years of social transition to which he was witness.

Later Waugh revolted against the book. Is it not included, and condemned, in the piece of literary history which he slips into *The End of the Battle?*—not quite Ludovic's "very gorgeous, almost gaudy, tale of romance and high drama," but almost certainly one of those "books which would turn from drab alleys of the thirties into the odorous gardens of a recent past transformed and illuminated by disordered memory and imagination." And, certainly, Waugh wrote nothing more in the *Brideshead* style. He recoiled to speed and pungency. Evidently he felt that there was fulsomeness in *Brideshead*'s nostalgic tone and baroque ornamentation, and that its conservative rhetoric, though apparently proper in a chronicle which describes, and makes us like, the conservative art of Ryder, was peacockish. And he may have felt that sentiment had broken out of its containing form.

At this point a word may be said on Waugh's sentiment in general. Sentiment is not always so vicious as the academies suppose. The Victorians, from Dickens to Louisa May Alcott, did very well with the conglomerations of event and emotion which make us "laugh and cry." Waugh sometimes practices their sequences, in his own fashion. So does Joyce. Joyce kept in sight a rule of that anti-Dickensian Meredith: "The sentimentalist is he who would enjoy without incurring the immense debtorship for a thing done." Intended as a stricture, the sentence implies, as Joyce saw, a positive corollary: pay the immense debt and you are entitled to the enjoyment. Joyce paid with a lifetime of labour, the intellectuality of his architecture, his own health and his family's (losing parts while he wrote, like Captain Carpenter dropping limbs while he rode).

Waugh paid with stylistic severities, structural economy, a
ruthless demeanour and illiberal inventions like the Connolly
children, by which he made himself to some a public enemy
and to himself a poor representative of his religion ("Why does
everyone except me find it so easy to be nice?" groans Pinfold).
Having paid, he permitted himself a lachryma, a tableau, a
carillon, an arabesque of paling stars, but at distant intervals
and briefly. They were indulgences which, though he had
worked for them honestly, he eyed sternly. He struggled, life-
long, to keep his sentiment prisoner and earn its parole. In
Brideshead the sentiment ran free and wild. Or so it seemed
to him when he eventually looked at the print. Never again!

It is bad taste to like *Brideshead*. I like it. For all its blem-
ishes, the soft places, the pompous antitheses in the Churchill
mode, the incredibly unoriginal "epic similes" of kingfisher
and Chinese ivory, it moves with a compelling flight. It records a social change, and Waugh's pain for the slipping past,
his disgust with a present "where wealth is no longer gorgeous
and power has no dignity." It takes up the questions of *A
Handful of Dust* again: reconsiders and praises again the great-
house and responsible-family values of Young England; re-
sumes and extends the moral study, this time, however, not
with a sombre and Puritanical condemnation of frivolity, but
with a voluptuous catalogue of the beauties of house and foun-
tain, wines and food, men and girls, and a testimony to the
sweetness of these first gods of his, in virtue of which his re-
nunciation becomes the greater. As Sebastian's story, the subject of *Brideshead* is the making of a saint, and it has a place
beside other books of the first half of our century which have
the same subject: Ford's *Fifth Queen* and his Tietjens series,
Eliot's *Cocktail Party*, Greene's *Power and the Glory* and *A
Burnt-Out Case*. As the story of a house and a family, it is a
parable of the struggle of England (in whose skies, said the
Fifth Queen, the angels weep) for the end of infidelity and the
reconnection with faith. As Ryder's story, it is the drama of

78 the artist—George Herbert's drama, for instance, as well as Waugh's—pulled between Beauty and God.

It is horrible and excellent by its repudiation of love. After her marriage to the coarse Rex Mottram and one or two will-o'-the-wisp affairs Julia Brideshead finds passionate love with Ryder. It is a joy. She fights to keep it. She gives it up on the edification of her father's unpredictably religious death. She sends Ryder away. Sends him away because she loves him and while she admits that sooner or later she will be in bed with someone else. But a "jolly-up," as Waugh's Mayfair slang puts it, is superficial and venial. Love for Ryder, standing between her and God, is indefensible. Graham Greene plots *The End of the Affair* in a similar way. In contradistinction to the romantic and market-place dogma, according to which carnality is sanctioned by sincere love, the neo-Catholic novel says that lust does less harm than love, which induces forgetfulness of God. But where there is love the lover will sooner or later be confronted with a crucial opportunity to foreswear it. Julia lays hold on the opportunity. Ryder leaves Brideshead, telling Julia in his grim to-the-point style that he hopes her heart will break. But he learns that she made the right choice, by which, as the epilogue implies with a neat restraint, he too is directed to God. This is a peculiar twisting of the old concept of the Christian Platonists that beauty and love are a ladder: the *scala al Fattor*. They may be; but on condition that they are sacrificed.

Is love one of Waugh's aversions? A choric paean in *Work Suspended* does obeisance to "love that delights in weakness, seeks out and fills the empty places and completes itself in its work of completion." *Brideshead*, his fullest study of passion, praises and deplores it. His other stories are busier with the pleasures of fornication in which emotions never play or only lightly. Whereas Greene talks in almost every novel about the ambush and pathos of love.

In *Brideshead* Waugh's binary pattern is lop-sided: much more attention is given to figures of affection and honour than to figures of inanity and malevolence. But there is a studied attack on the Modern Age that takes the great house over and deforms it. Waugh projects the modern spirit in two persons: the raw Hooper, dealt with in a few strokes; Rex Mottram, drawn more exactly to catch the insentience, the gaping lacuna, beneath the bombast. Mottram has a virtue: the enterprising courage with which he made his first ten thousand pounds. But his enterprise aims at crude ends by rotten means. His ear is alert for news of "mortal illness and debt." He has no curiosity about meaning, no sense of tradition, responsibility, or the charities. It is a gloomy paradox of the war that Mottram becomes a Cabinet Minister. A victory with and for him may be a defeat. This point, thrust into the last pages of the book, adumbrates Waugh's profound pessimism: there will never be much decency in the res publica, never much relief from folly and violence.

Waugh is honest. Whether he likes a thing or not, he reports it; whether we are going to like it or not, he reports it. *Brideshead* is an honest political chronicle. Ryder participates in the General Strike of 1926. He volunteers, as Waugh had volunteered, to patrol the streets of London in a self-appointed posse of playboy deputies and cudgel the workmen, whom he expects to see storming some Bastille and letting riot loose. For Ryder and Waugh working-people and democracy mean the sans-culottes and the mob, and the mob means the sacking of order and beauty and the death of Christ. But that is in the streets of the imagination. In the streets of London Ryder is surprised by normalcy, his team gets no "good battle," and its sole victim is, by the muddle of these occasions, a man of peace. Yet when the Strike is called off he feels "as though a beast long fabled for its ferocity had emerged for an hour, scented danger, and slunk back to its lair." Such is his nightmare. On the other hand, he catches the nullity of the aristocratic strike-breakers in a dozen lines of drunken dialogue. More significantly, he shows Lord Brideshead refusing to rally to his caste: "Brideshead had re-

80 fused to take any public service because he was not satisfied with the justice of the cause." As a man Brideshead is pedantic and absurd, but as a Catholic he is incorruptibly serious. Eighteen years after 1926 Waugh admits, what he could not have admitted then, that to a religious man who tests every act of his life and every public event by the principles of his faith, the ancien régime is sometimes wrong, the people sometimes right. For a moment he makes touch with the actively egalitarian Catholicism, which was heard in Chesterton (consider his sonnet, "I Know You") and is heard often today.

The plot of *Brideshead* moves through a sequence of change comparable to the change which took place in Waugh's art across his thirty-five writing years. The charm of Ryder at Oxford yields to the leanness of the later Ryder, the ripple of beauty to the solemnity of conviction, the sunniness of morning to a darkness centuries old, world-wide, lit by a lamp. In the latter half of this book, and perhaps hardly anywhere else in Waugh, unless in the rather different *Helena*, the religious sensibility is allowed expression in a poetic modulating of the prose, in a dark flickering, in bars of diapason. There is some intuition of the continuity from Judaism to Christianity: " 'You've never been to Tenebrae, I suppose?' 'Never.' 'Well, if you had you'd know what the Jews felt about their temple. *Quomodo sedet sola civitas* . . . .' " There are suggestions of the "catholicism" of the Church: "All over the world people were on their knees . . . ." ". . . *Quomodo sedet sola civitas* . . . I had heard that great lament . . . sung by a half-caste choir in Guatemala." Over-rich, Waugh afterwards felt, and did it no more. But good that he did it once!

By two post-war sallies, *Scott-King's Modern Europe* and *The Loved One* (Dennis Barlow's Modern California), Waugh proves to himself that he is not lost in his emotions: that he can still write rapidly. He demonstrates the feat of reducing a novel to a novella. He had once complimented his fictitious Ambrose Silk on "a story which a popular writer would have spun out to 150,000 words; Ambrose missed nothing; it was all there, delicately and precisely, in fifty pages." He enjoys his own prowess.

Both tales are rejections of the modern world, to fit a boy for which "would be very wicked indeed." Both performances are equally expert. *The Loved One* has eclipsed *Scott-King* only because its mortuary details evoke that lugubrious public giggling which increases as the formal religions disintegrate, or, as Ludovic would claim, with our "death-wish."

Elaborated with the same economy, *Helena* is an offering: a Catholic's offering to the Church which received him; a pilgrim's offering to the saint who travelled from the Home Counties to Jerusalem; a middle-aged man's offering to the boy who went to Oxford as a History Scholar; an Englishman's offering to Britain. He chooses, for this history of the making of a saint, a British saint, and suggests with a free fancy and a spice of convinced enthusiasm that England has contributed not only to the roll of saints but to the traditions and outlook of the Church. Helena found in Christianity what no other creed of her time could offer, the history of a man who lived, taught, and died, and rituals which involved the Christian in the experience: this is His body, this is His blood. She embraced a religion intelligible to her British pragmatism; and by seeking and finding the Cross she helped to confirm and perpetuate the three-dimensional realism of the Church. And she brought British humour to Roman gravity, the fresh-air dash of the hunting-field and the tenacious British equestrians to the recovery of relics and the Catholic temper, the earthiness of the Colchester stables to a faith born in a stable. Waugh knows how far too far he is going; but it is a piece of English humour to make a wholly genuine, wholly humble oblation with these impossible flourishes. He offers, in fact, a toy. At the close he invokes the Magi: they were late-comers, and are therefore patrons for a convert, and they brought exotic toys as their gifts, and are

82   therefore patrons for artists and lapidary writers: "pray
always for all the learned, the oblique, the delicate. Let them
not be quite forgotten at the Throne of God when the simple
come into their kingdom."

In small but not negligible part *Helena* is also a satire on
Roman politics; and the lurid gibes enable us to see more
clearly into Waugh's novels and the man. We understand the
name of Prime Minister Outrage. We understand why Pinfold
has never voted in a Parliamentary election, and why he has
even abstained from the Catholic efforts to go from the rock
to the forum and redeem the times. Waugh believes that
political life has always been polluted. Mottram had his
counterparts in the Roman warlords, climbing to the purple
over strangled competitors and bartered wives. If "history"
means "the sequence of politics," then Waugh says, as Helena
says to her heedless son, "Keep out of history"—words in tune
with the Joycean "History is a nightmare from which I am
trying to awake." The Empire, the City, the Bureau, all collective undertakings, are contaminated. Pull out to a Dalmatian
farm or a house in the Cotswolds. This political dismay is not
unique, but Waugh's cry of retreat is. Among the English
writers in general, and the neo-Catholic writers certainly, the
tendency is to regard politicians as corrupt (landsmen
scoundrels, growled Conrad), yet to hold it the staple of
honour to remain engaged and struggle with corruption. Ford
knew the facts of politics, was near the pre-1914 Establishment when scandal battered it, later saw the profiteers in the
lunch-cars of the wartime trains and wrote his angry verse-
commentary, *Footsloggers*; but he persevered with the notion
of a clean society; and he recalls in *Parade's End* not only the
viciousness of his rulers but the goodwill he has sometimes
encountered in them. The High Tory Tietjens and the Radical
Cabinet Minister (modelled on C.F.G. Masterman) get together over a beer and agree "on two fundamental legislative
ideals: every working man to have a minimum of four hundred

pounds a year and every beastly manufacturer who wanted to
pay less to be hung." Graham Greene, who took his inspiration
from Ford, combs politics to find good men in Sodom and finds
them: Dr. Magiot in Haiti, and the Wisconsin Presidential
Candidate, and the Candidate's wife: by whose constancy the
world may be redeemed. Eliot urged that, while the first problem is to learn the right theology, the next is to apply it to the
cleansing of the State and the struggle, not to be refused
though the end is beyond achievement, for the City of God
on earth. So Waugh stands apart from the predecessors and
contemporaries who otherwise are nearest to him.

But he is in touch with a different tradition. He has one
prescription for the improvement of the world: cultivate.
Helena tells her son to do the work she has done on her lands:
"clearing and draining and planting. That is something better
than history." Swift, amid his furious indictment of man's mis-
conduct and madness, rather similarly said: "whoever could
make two ears of corn or two blades of grass to grow upon a
spot of ground where only one grew before, would deserve
better of mankind and do more essential service to his country
than the whole race of politicians put together." We may also
think of Lord Munodi in Balnibarbi, or Pope's tribute to
Bathurst.

A disappointment at its first appearance, *The Ordeal of
Gilbert Pinfold* now begins to seem a little masterpiece, and
is an indispensable source for any study of Waugh. He must
have known how it could be used to analyse him. But it was
a drama lived in him, given to him complete, and, with his
artist's sense of the relevance of the object, he would not abjure
it. The experience was medical and religious (is there any
difference?). In an old language: Pinfold is possessed by de-
mons. In the current language: impulses suppressed under the
carefully-practised persona of the Cotswold Tory demand a
hearing. A "hearing" is the exact word. Pinfold's hallucina-
tions are aural. The anarchists and rioters, whom Waugh once

84 evoked as performers on his page and who seemed satisfied with that *Lebensraum*, now rebel against some insufficiency of attention and get beyond his management. They separate from his pen and speak, with thoroughly-realised identities, as if in a neighbouring but impenetrable room, or over a radio which he cannot switch off. They accuse him of the faults his prejudices and convictions most resent. He stands blazoned as his own enemy, his own victim. *Pinfold* is a *Dorian Gray*, but the conception is truer, the execution more naturalistic, the purpose a scrupulous fact-finding.

Across the span of the fifties Waugh composed a trilogy in which he brought together his several modes, informative reporting, comic fantasy, angry satire, sentimental admiration, and a nostalgia which is carefully moderated to avoid the *Brideshead* baroque. And the trilogy is more than a mosaic of styles. In this final sustained effort the impudent inventions of his farces and the pudor and predication of his moralities are blended.

The trilogy is the story of Guy Crouchback's quest for the reason of his creation, the story of the making of his soul. It is also—and the mating is superb—the story of his War: why he enlisted; what he hoped; what he suffered. *Men-at-Arms* begins in a mood of promise, almost of soaring. Guy has spent the thirties in comfortable but pointless isolation and sloth, for which he blames himself, and from which the War, surely a Crusade against the shames of the modern world, brings release. He hurries to England to play his part, and is accepted by the Halberdiers. For two hundred pages of pleasant fantasy and neat reporting Waugh describes his "love-affair" with the Army, his initiation into Halberdier etiquette, oddities, and decencies. Then, in the last five chapters, a slow reversal begins: on an African beach Guy leads his first raid competently, but gets a reprimand instead of a citation. Within a month his friendly gift of whisky accelerates Apthorpe's

death, and he gets a rocket. We are descending to the dark
mood of the second novel of the trilogy.

Officers and Gentlemen is a book of anger. Though there
is a glimpse of Churchill, a Waugh hero, cutting through disorder with robust commonsense, it is a-typical. By and large,
the tale is of the termites—incompetence, nest-feathering, and
something like treason—which tunnel official structures.
There is the mess and malice of the real Crusades, little of the
chivalry of the Crusades of legend.

The nouns of the title ring satirically. We have been thinking of Waugh, he has thought of himself, as a champion of
caste. He springs surprises. Not in Trimmer, who is Waugh's
New Man as we might have expected him to be, guileful,
cheap, and oafish. But in some of the minor characters who
rave and madden through his pages. In Ludovic, the New
Writer. Ludovic is out of the mould of the Admirable Crichton.
He has the skills of the Barrie–Wodehouse butler, rooted in
the resourcefulness of primitive man. He has the butler's
deference. Break through the deference, and you may hear a
snarl. For Pinfold Waugh there is nothing nastier than "the
underdog's snarl." Waugh of the trilogy is ambivalent. When
the friction between the vicious overdog, Major Hound, and
the underdog Ludovic comes to ignition-point in a cave in
Crete, Ludovic's deferential voice ("after what's happened,
Sir, don't you think it will be more suitable") suddenly turns
from its plummy to the plebeian key ("to shut your bloody
trap"). Waugh immediately throws in an image of bats burst-
ing down from the vault of the cave, reminiscent of the "beast"
of the General Strike. But Ludovic's bite at the hound has already set us cheering; the bats hardly frighten us; and we remain cheerful when the Mob in the shape of Ludovic guil-
lotines Authority in the shape of the Major.

Less vivid but curiously significant is the case of Ivor Claire.
Waugh's introductory picture of this officer, elegant, quiet

86 and contained, impeccably taking his horse over jumps, suggests that he is to be a symbol of aristocratic dependability and that the Allied triumph will be a triumph of blue blood. Guy looks at him and perceives "quintessential England, the man Hitler had not taken into account." But Waugh is preparing a turn-about that no reader of his previous novels would have dared to predict. Quietly and adroitly Claire rats in Crete. He leaves his troops and brother-officers to fall prisoner and makes a comparatively cosy evacuation. It is one of the disillusions with which Waugh conducts Guy's sentimental education. And the next? The Establishment rallies round Claire, covers his disgrace, and ships Guy, who might have given evidence against him, by slowest transport home. The Angry writers have written, of course, more boisterously and blisteringly against the Establishment, but these rapid pages of *Officers and Gentlemen* sharply expose its *mores* and manoeuvres; and they have the value of in-criticism: Waugh lams his own group at the bidding of fact and justice. This is the positive side of his cult of eccentricity. When the Establishment says "Hush," he's damned if he'll hush.

All the same, Waugh likes Claire—and what he stands for—too much to leave him in permanent disgrace, and, reverting to an Imperial convention, he arranges for him to win back his spurs in Burma. Here and elsewhere the trilogy quivers under the oscillation between a mature and an immature Waugh. (This is not a literary fault. An unstable position may be fearfully interesting.)

The title of the British edition of the third novel of the trilogy is *Unconditional Surrender*, of the American, *The End of the Battle*. It is a pun in both languages: the enemy "unconditionally surrenders," Guy conforms to the will of God; the war ends in a victory, Guy's inner struggle ends in reconciliation with God. Throughout the pages Guy continues to suffer the sour defeats that the world thrusts on a good man. Like Tietjens in *Parade's End*, which in several respects is the

War I equivalent of this War II trilogy, he finds that anything
brave, competent, or humane he does in his crusading goes
down on the official dossiers to his discredit. Is it possible to
remain uncorrupted by disillusionment? Under the volley of
perplexities Guy learns, like the tragic heroes, to know himself and others. He learns that war and its attendants come
when everyone in some measure wills them; and that even
the man who welcomes war for an honourable reason, to drive
off his own sloth in driving out an evil system, is among the
guilty. " 'God forgive me', said Guy, 'I was one of them'." He
also finds his way, like a comic hero, to success: a religious
success, for this is a religious comedy. He performs the "small
service which only he could perform, for which he had been
created." He belongs to a distinguished Catholic house. The
gallantry of gentlemen and the courage of martyrs is represented in its annals; it stands for courtesy, humility, and
charity. He is the last heir and has no child and his wife is
estranged. Now his wife becomes pregnant, but not by him:
by Trimmer, the representative of democracy, "the people's
war," and push. Guy remarries her in full knowledge of the
circumstances. Commonsense and fair play, in the person of
his Scottish friend, Kerstie, try to stop him: " 'You poor
bloody fool', said Kerstie, anger and pity and something near
love in her voice, 'you're being *chivalrous*—about *Virginia*.
Can't you understand men aren't chivalrous any more and
I don't believe they ever were'." Guy makes his choice with
a Young England chivalry and a Catholic care for the soul
that transcends questions of dignity or pedigree. His father
has taught him, in a letter which is the heart of the book, that
"the Church . . . doesn't strike attitudes and stand on its
dignity. It accepts suffering and injustice." There may be
danger in this non-militant doctrine. But how beautifully
Waugh presents and applies it! The invention of the parable
of Virginia's child and Guy's acceptance is Waugh's unconditional surrender. He has fought the modern world, hated

88 the people in their raw emergence. But now he accepts the crossing of the strains and takes the child of the sans-culottes into the gentle heritage. The old England accepts the new England. It is a sacrifice; Waugh has made Trimmer unmitigatedly gross so that no reader can call the decision less than a sacrifice. The immolation of Waugh's dream of past and caste is Isaac burned: intolerable, magnificent.

Lonely socialite, grim gay-dog, curmudgeon of the gospel of mercy, Waugh loved the stance of the Retrograde, sulkily barring his Church from its heartening resumption of the social tasks of Christianity. But as we read him we are likely to find, to our surprise, and, were he here, to his, and to our pleasure, but it would not have been to his, that he was a nicer man than he thought. On the evidence of the trilogy we must say at the very least, that if he was too much of a snob to accept redbrick England like a gentleman (old Mr. Crouchback would have done better, and Jimmy Porter's father-in-law did better), he was religious enough to take it as his Cross.

"The men loved him. He made them laugh." Graham Greene writes this epitaph for Jones—who is almost Apthorpe. *The Comedians* is, indeed, finely sprayed with reminiscences of Waugh's fiction, and seems to say that in a world of grit and violence (and Greene generally has embodied the grit and violence much better than Waugh) comedy represents and begets courage and sparkles with consolation (and Waugh generally has animated and consoled the world better than Greene). If there were nothing else in Waugh but the absurd inventions, the wit, the slang poetry, he would command our affection and gratitude. But there is more: the reporting of his time, the fierce individual reaction to it, the struggle with a conscience strengthening against his will, the resolute moralizing of his tale at the cost of popularity. And there is the tenacity with which he laboured to make his light novels works of art. He *was* an artist. He wrote because he must— because his imagination stepped beyond the permitted into unpermitted zones. But even the authentic writer who writes because he must may write carelessly. Waugh wrote as trenchantly as he could. And "if he pleased, he pleased by manly ways." We are in his debt alike for his comedy, for the moralities which are the annals of the civil war in his soul, and for his craftsmanship.

5

Robert Boyle, S.J.

To Look Outside:
The Fiction of J. F. Powers

In *Commentary*, July 1965, J. F. Powers wrote a review of *In Solitary Witness: the Life and Death of Franz Jäger-stätter*, by Gordon Zahn. Powers's treatment of this study of a Christian martyred by the Nazis revealed some of his own principal interests: the solitary witness, the individual standing by his principles in spite of his world, e.g., his refusal to serve in a war he judges unjust; the relationship between an individual and God; and the relationship between an individual and his church. Jägerstätter was, like Powers, a Catholic, and Powers glances at the "miserable works and acts" of the German hierarchy, which in his view evidently failed to live up to its own commitment, and whose failure, Powers emotionally states, makes it "hard not to despair."

But most of all, the mystery of Jägerstätter's motivation is rooted in his belief and love: "What nobody in this book seemed to understand at the time, perhaps not even Jägerstät-ter, was that *he* believed in God and the hereafter as others didn't—and could afford to live and die as others couldn't." In this profound region, where reason can peer but not penetrate, can be found the secret of man's puzzling operation. Shake-speare advances the same notion several times, notably in

Robert Boyle, S.J.

92 Sonnet 116, when he indicates that love ("whose worth's unknown") can alone give meaning to human life and to literature:

> If this be error and upon me proved,
> I never writ, nor no man ever loved.

And in *A Midsummer Night's Dream*, IV, 1, in paraphrasing St. Paul, I Corinthians, 2, Shakespeare insinuates through Bottom that the love of human for human is analogous to the incomprehensible love of God for each human individual. As I see it, Powers as a literary artist operates on a basis similar to Shakespeare's, and sees love and hate as the primary determining forces in all human affairs.

In Powers's vision of reality, then, each individual is what he chooses to be. Powers sees humans capable of choosing to love or to hate, and, ultimately, freely choosing to do so. By no means does he neglect the complex determining forces an individual's society presses upon him, but he shows clearly and distinctly that these forces are not ultimates. For example, in "The Forks," from *Prince of Darkness and Other Stories* (1958), Father Eudex has the whole force of his world, ecclesiastical in the person of Msgr. Sweeney, secular in the collectivity of the Rival Company, bearing upon him to relax his own principles of self-respect, to accept the money and the manners of others, and thus to conform comfortably to the world around him. As Father Eudex sees it, he is invited to serve both God and Mammon, and his struggle ends with his flushing the inviting check down the toilet. The story concludes with Father Eudex's imagining the Last Judgment, with all his confreres stating the good Christian things they did with their checks, and finally poses what is for him the cosmic question: "And you, Father?" In the implicit and equally cosmic answer, the toilet is symbolically elevated to an unaccustomed supernatural service. And the lonely individual, the solitary witness, withstands, in all his ironic and comic littleness, the forces of evil.

In the tender, deeply moving "The Old Bird, A Love Story," Mr. Newman is finally presented with a choice between sticking to fact, the harsh truth that the miserable Christmas job he has secured is only temporary, and assenting, for his wife's sake, to the illusion that the job will last. He has always insisted on being a realist, on dealing, like his hierarchical namesake, with reality as he finds it. But at last, like the dying Desdemona, he can because of love close his eyes to the surface truth and through love, see in the human spirit something deeper than fact. Love here survives the passing of "rosy lips and cheeks" and "bears it out even to the edge of doom." Once again, in showing the choice made by a loving individual, Powers subtly and profoundly points toward the mystery of the human spirit in operation.

In one of his most effective stories, "Prince of Darkness," Powers addresses himself to the struggle between the actual and the ideal in a priest. The title, a traditional appellation of Satan, possibly refers to Edgar's defense of the devil in *King Lear*, III, 4, 141: "The prince of darkness is a gentleman." Powers, like Joyce and other literary artists, has a penchant for using his titles to give his stories a large, suggestive, and illuminating context. Here we are prepared for seeing Father Burner as a devil, or an instrument of Satan, but we may find a defense of him, too, and no condemnation. Indeed, as we get more and more involved in the details of Burner's life, in his crude and insensitive treatment of penitents, in his petty vanities, in his background and opinions, in the attitudes his colleagues adopt toward him, in his pitifully limited hopes, we understand and even sympathize with him more and more, until we almost hope that the Bishop's envelope will reveal what we know it should not. We know at the end that he is not a good priest, but we have witnessed his ineffectual

94 attempts to be a gentleman. His ultimate choice, it would appear, is or will be, probably, himself rather than another; he will hate the outside world rather than love it, selfishly willing his own good rather than that of any other. Thus, apparently, he really is a subject of the Prince of Darkness, as Stephen Dedalus strove to be. But not certainly so. A mysterious ambiguity remains. And Powers leaves it so, showing us what can be seen and leaving the vital mystery shrouded in the mists of reality itself. Certainly Burner's ultimate choice is operative, and it appears that it must be the free choice of self rather than of the good outside. But Burner does not see this, nor, finally, do we. We see only the impenetrable mystery of the human spirit in concrete operation.

Powers's interest in the hierarchy of the Catholic Church appears in most of his work. He observes what happens to human beings when they get involved in so large and complicated an institution, when they are drawn by divine as well as by human commitments.

In "The Keystone," which appeared in *The New Yorker* for May 18, 1963, we see a bishop tyrannized over by his ambitious underlings. John Dullinger, Bishop of Ostergothenburg, and a character in *Morte d'Urban*, builds a new cathedral; in the process the politics of the clergy, the humanity involved in the construction, the relations with the laity, the relations with nature (chiefly with cats, favorite rectory creatures with Powers) are subtly and comically depicted. The decline of Msgr. Holstein and the rise of Father (Msgr., Bishop-elect) Gau, who is most perfectly characterized in one word, "Gee," give a background to the efforts, hopes, and limitations of the bishop. The characterization is not profound, but in its implications it is enormously broad, and it sympathetically reflects the humanity of the Church without in any way minimizing its divinity. It is, in other words, a true artist's vision of the hierarchy in operation.

In "Dawn," the first story in *The Presence of Grace* (1962),

and one perhaps left over from the building of *Morte*
d'Urban, we find the bishop and his chancellor involved in
the conventional red tape inevitable in a monarchical institution like the Catholic Church. A personal note to the pope appears, sealed, in the annual Peter's Pence collection; Msgr.
Renton (Urban Roche's friend), hoping to make trouble for
Father Udovic, the chancellor, whom he dislikes, sends it on
to the chancery instead of opening it as he normally would
have done. As the matter rises from the lowly housekeeper
who counted the collection through the curates and the pastor
to the chancellor and thence to the bishop, it gathers an importance like that Alexander Pope celebrates for the ringlet
in *The Rape of the Lock*. The story centers in Father Udovic,
who at the end sees himself in the hell he occupies with Mrs.
Anton, the sender of the letter. She is greedy, small-souled,
contemptuous of flunkies. Father Udovic perceives this, and
in a flash of self-knowledge not unlike that experienced by
Father Urban in *Morte d'Urban*, realizes that he, like Mrs.
Anton, has acted from selfish and unworthy motives, not at
all out of love for the pope and the Church, but out of a convention masking greed and contempt. He had sounded his own
trumpet as loudly as he could until trapped by the woman who
used his own scheme against him by sounding hers. It is a
sympathetic and compassionate, as well as comic, vision which
Powers here presents of the hierarchy, ordinary humans who
must act in a demanding suprahuman milieu.

   In "A Losing Game" and "The Presence of Grace," we see
a Christlike pastor[1] indirectly through the eyes of his curate.
Father Fabre, the curate, loses the game in the first story because he tries to play according to the eccentric rules of his odd
pastor without realizing the pastor's true, concealed charity.
In the second story, where the absence of Grace, one of the
members of the Altar and Rosary Society, compromises Father
Fabre quite badly in a touchy social situation, Father Fabre,
suffering the women's attack, would, left to himself, counter-

96 attack with the women's own weapons—suppositions and words. The pastor simply refuses to accept the attack, tenaciously denying the validity of their suppositions, and herding them like sheep, with an effective and almost wordless love, into true charity. He symbolically uses his stick only to open the church windows, thus letting into the midst of his harried flock the fresh air of Christian good will.

In "The Lord's Day," from *Prince of Darkness*, we see quite a different pastor, thoughtless, inconsiderate, even tyrannical. We see him in this instance through the eyes of the superior of the parish nuns. The story deals with the struggle between the pastor and the superior over the survival of the one tree he has left to them, and the pastor wins. But the struggle reveals a great deal about both of them. It would on the surface appear that the difficulties rise from the defects in the pastor, but a careful consideration of the details of the story uncovers the pride, the self-conscious concerns, the conventional attitudes of the nun. Finally one perceives that had she not acted from human respect, from cowardice, and from refusal to deal with the pastor in kind and realistic terms, as another of the nuns might have done, the situation would not have developed. The human struggles in the hierarchy, based in the individual's own free choice of love or hate, of self or another, here stem from the nun's own lack of Christian love.

Another aspect of the hierarchy's problems appears in "The Valiant Woman." In this story the pastor is tyrannized by his housekeeper. Once again the title, drawn from Proverbs 31:10, "Who shall find a valiant woman," and liturgically from the Mass common to holy women not martyrs, gives a large and ironic context to the story. The struggle for mastery between Father Firman and Mrs. Stoner has clearly been won by Mrs. Stoner long before the story begins. It is the clerical version of the battle of the sexes. The hierarchy does not escape it, and Powers shows us in Father Firman a reed not firm, but indeed one almost totally destroyed by the psychic stones of his

ruthless companion. He has only enough strength left to lunge
at a symbolic female mosquito.

But we reach the depths of Powers's interests when we observe his treatment of belief and love. In "Jamesie," surely a largely autobiographical study of youthful disillusionment comparable to Joyce's "Araby," the boy loves and admires the local team's pitcher, Lefty. Jamesie has abandoned the middle-class culture of the Illinois town in which he grew up for the romantic world of Baseball Bill and Tom Swift, heroes who face and conquer evil, who make things turn out right. The boy's illusion is finally shattered by his realization of evil in his hero. "He used the streets and sidewalks, like anyone else, to get where he was going—away—and was not quite himself." That final sentence reveals the individual, driven out of his romantic Eden, sinking into the conventions of his society "like anyone else." Belief in a human ideal and love for a hero have withered beneath the knowledge of Lefty's weakness and cupidity, and the ten-year-old must return to a world in which things "turned out wrong."

In "The Trouble," which deals with a Southern race riot as seen through the eyes of a Negro child, the struggle between hate and love centers in the Negro father. The suffering of the innocent, the religious faith of the grandmother, the cowardice of the white Catholic, although important elements of the story, merely contribute to the vital moment when the father, driven to an ultimate choice, turns from his wife's beaten and dead body and says to the white man "in the stillest kind of a whisper, 'I wouldn't touch you.'" His self-respect, his "black belief," win out over all the forces of evil brought to bear upon him, and the grandmother's "Jesus" intimates a connection between the Negro father and Christ. The father *would* not hate, and thus reveals another aspect of human love.

Powers depicts the nature of love most powerfully in "Lions, Harts, Leaping Does." The old Franciscan priest Didymus, not far from death, questions with scrupulous intensity the faith

98 he has striven to live for his ninety or so years. Bogged down in exegesis, as the title of the story suggests, he fluctuates between the irascible (the lions) and concupiscible (the harts and does) powers of the soul. His simple-minded companion, Brother Titus, ordered to read from any book, takes down John of the Cross's *Spiritual Canticle of the Soul*, and starts reading the saint's turgid discussion of the scholastic exegesis of his poem. Didymus breaks in weakly, "Skip the exegesis. I can do without that now. Read the verse." Now, at long last, Didymus is ready to break through the human complications, the mazes of his faulty and self-centered belief, and, like Urban Roche after him, to go directly to the simple and beautiful text of divinized reality itself.

After Didymus suffers a paralyzing stroke, the devoted Titus brings a canary to keep him company. The caged bird becomes for Didymus (as a caged skylark did for Hopkins) a symbol of the spirit. At the climax of the story, when Didymus at last, almost in his moment of death, dies to himself, the bird, released by Didymus, escapes into the snowy garden. Titus, standing at the open window, too good to lie, too lovingly considerate to let Didymus know that the bird has escaped, fusses with the window-latch. Didymus, watching Titus's dilemma, at last learns, in the midst of his tense and futile efforts to find God, what he must do to be saved. Like Titus, he too must unselfconsciously love another. Simple Titus, looking out in concern for the bird, dissimulating out of concern for Didymus, totally selfless, manifests God to Didymus: "He [Didymus] knew he still had to look outside, to Titus. God still chose to manifest Himself most in sanctity." Not in intellectual superiority, but in simple love, in looking outside, in the unselfish willing of good to another, is God achieved.

Two aspects of Powers's technique contribute powerfully to his expression of his vision of reality, his rhythms, and his symbols. The delicacy and accuracy of his ear can be observed

on every page of his work. Two examples will serve here, both
from "He Don't Plant Cotton," Powers's first published story,
which appeared in *Accent* in 1943. The story deals with a
group of Negro musicians, and, imaginatively entering into the
mind and background of the drummer (modelled after Baby
Dodds), Powers reproduces the thoughts and rhythms that
go through the drummer's mind: "New York may be all right,
he hummed to himself, but Beale Street's paved with gold.
That's a lie, he thought; I been down on Beale. And Chicago,
same way. All my life playing jobs in Chicago, and I still got
to ride the Big Red. And that's no lie." A few pages later he
shifts easily to reflect the rhythms and emotions of the piano
player:

And Libby was pleased, watching Baby. And then, somehow,
he vanished for her into the blue drum. The sticks still danced
at an oblique angle on the snare, but there were no hands to
them and Libby could not see Baby on the chair. She could only
feel him somewhere in the blue glow. Abandoning herself, she
lost herself in the piano. Now, still without seeing him, she
could feel him with a clarity and warmth beyond vision.
Miniature bell notes, mostly blue, blossomed ecstatically,
perished *affettuoso*, weaving themselves down into the dark
beauty of the lower keys, because it was closer to the drum, and
multiplied.

Powers handles symbols with effortless ease. He does not,
at least not usually, impose them upon his material, but lets
them spring up, or seem to, from the matter with which he
deals. The money in "The Lord's Day" indeed suggests in
several ways the "filthy lucre" of St. Paul and the pieces of
silver which tempted Judas. The snow in "Lions, Harts, Leaping Does," as in Joyce's "The Dead," symbolizes death,
though in a way different from Joyce's. In Joyce the symbol
is richly ambiguous, stressing the passion of Christ but not
explicitly ruling out the resurrection; in Powers, it is more
simply dealt with, suggesting the reception both of the bird

and of the spirit of Didymus into "the snowy arms of God." In "The Forks," forks become the symbol of culture, refinement, gentlemanliness as viewed by the Monsignor, and of Pharisaical hypocrisy as viewed by Father Eudex. The mosquito in "The Valiant Woman"—as close as Powers comes to imposing a symbol on his material—symbolizes the bloodsucking female.

No detail escapes Powers's careful imagination. The density of his ubiquitous symbolic interest may be observed in this passage from "Prince of Darkness." Father Burner, looking for his aviator's helmet (Milton's Prince of Darkness also flew) in his crowded closet, finds a golf ball, a Royal Bomber:

He stuck the helmet on his balding head to get it out of the way and took the putter from the bag. He dropped the ball at the door of the closet. Taking his own eccentric stance—a perversion of what the pro recommended and a dozen books on the subject—he putted the ball across the room at a dirty collar lying against the bookcase. A thready place in the carpet caused the ball to jump the collar and to loose a pamphlet from the top of the bookcase. He restored the pamphlet—Pius XI on "Atheistic Communism"—and poked the ball back to the door of the closet. Then, allowing for the carpet, he drove the ball straight, *click*, through the collar, *clop*. Still had his old putting eye. And his irons had always been steady if not exactly crashing. It was his woods, the tee shots, that ruined his game. He'd give a lot to be able to hit his woods properly, not to dub his drives, if only on the first tee—where there was always a crowd (mixed).

Explicit is the mess of Father Burner's life: the collar on the floor, the bookcase so piled with pamphlets that the ball can jar one loose. Symbols imply much more. The collar, an obvious symbol of the priesthood used later in *Morte d'Urban*, is here dirty, and is subordinated to golf. Father Burner takes an eccentric stance, as, like Stephen Dedalus, he invariably insists upon doing, against all accumulated wisdom. The title

of the booklet—unread, the situation suggests, unlike the
dozen golf books—bolsters ,the impression that the evils of
Atheistic Communism are less impressive to Father Burner
than the failure of his tee shots. His inability to find the
straight and narrow path down the fairway stings him, but
mostly because others, especially women, see him fail.
Obviously Powers, like Joyce, like Shakespeare, like Hawthorne, implies and suggests through his symbols more than
he states about his characters.

An even more obvious and illuminating example of a complicated web of symbolism appears in a story previously referred to, "The Keystone." In a perceptive and valuable
analysis (*The Catholic World*, February 1964), John J. Kirvan,
C.S.P., who considers the symbols in this story obvious, almost crass, nevertheless suggests that we may learn a good
deal from it about Powers's procedure in his finer work, notably *Morte d'Urban*. I'm not certain that the symbols are as
crass as Father Kirvan thinks they are, but I deeply agree with
his conclusion that they are illuminating. The keystone image
is a favorite with the bishop in the story. At the opening, the
bishop is composing a pastoral letter: "The Bishop was about
to mention the keystone of authority, as he did so often in his
pastoral letters, that stone without which . . ." The clause is
not finished, but obviously will be something like "the arch
of the Church cannot stand." The bishop draws, obviously, on
the Scriptural image of Christ as keystone: "The Bishop continued: 'Did you never read this Scripture text: "The very
stone which the builders rejected has become the cornerstone
. . ." ' " (Matthew, 21:42). Christ Himself, in Catholic imagery,
is that necessary stone, and without Him there is no kingdom
of God. Father Kirvan notes the symbolism of the cathedral
church standing for the living Church (in Pauline imagery, 2
Corinthians, 6:16), with its special bond with Christ. In this
particular case the church building itself follows the secular
search for status by seeking out a "high-class residence only"

102 district; it is built not of fieldstones (ordinary people) but of prefinished stone veneer (Pharisees); it is held together, *not* by keystones, but by structural steel. Thus the organization, not the bishop as Christ's representative, becomes, Father Kirvan points out, the vital factor in holding things together. And this church, built on an old graveyard, is not for the ages but for "fifty, seventy-five—maybe a hundred years."

The principal symbol derives from the fact that the new cathedral's arches have no keystones. The architects, symbolically as well as really, wish to stress the vertical as against the horizontal. And Powers, perhaps too obviously, stresses the connection with the Gospel of Matthew in his diction: "Frank and Frank [the builders] had rejected keystones." Powers's picture of the American Catholic Church, as we see it in his symbolism, is of a structure built for modern times, without Christ, without the one necessary keystone which makes the whole building meaningful. Too much is made of the human vertical, and the divine horizontal disappears.

With this background, then, in Powers's subject matter and technique in his short stories, we may turn to his masterpiece, his only novel so far, *Morte d'Urban* (1962). The categories used above in examining his short stories—the individual, the hierarchy, and belief and love—may be useful here also. The individual, Urban Roche, impressed reviewers of the book in various ways. Martin Price, in *The Yale Review* (December 1962) found him "a man of great intelligence and urbane skill." Mr. Price also thought that Powers, "crassly punitive," makes Father Urban die "not in body, but in soul" at the end. And he considers the book "a series of nicely composed vignettes" rather than a novel. Thomas Curley, on the other hand, in *Commonweal* (October 12, 1962), states: "It would have surprised no one had the disciplines he mastered in the shorter form occasioned obvious faults in his novel. They did not, I think, because Powers so thoroughly realized the 'hero' of of his story, Father Urban Roche. . . . Morte d'Urban does not refer to the spiritual death of Urban Roche, but to the decline and 'death' of the character Urban, the glad-hander, the operator, the opportunist, the sucker for rich Catholics with a cruel streak in them. . . . Powers has managed an unusually subtle creation."

Mr. Curley's view of the matter is also mine. Powers starts in the midst of things, with Urban middle-aged, called upon to adapt to various new situations. Through flashbacks and through a series of revealing experiences, we follow Urban's knightly and apostolic career to a rather surprising conclusion, inevitable only if one has adverted to the deeper glimpses revealed in the symbolism that reflects Urban's spiritual development.

Powers uses as an epigraph a quotation from J. M. Barrie: "The life of every man is a diary in which he means to write one story, and writes another. . . ." The story Urban means to write we can see in his early idol, Father Placidus Hartigan. Father Placidus, as traveling preacher, won all hearts; he stayed at the hotel rather than the rectory, drove enthusiastically, and considered Benedict XV a saint, Belloc and Chesterton the great writers, the White Sox the best of teams. As provincial, he pushed athletics, created the Choristers, and, after a glorious three years, went back on the road. The knightly young Urban "had ridden into the dark wood of the parish-mission circuit alongside him and had sat next to him at the 'long count' Dempsey–Tunney fight where he suffered and concealed a seizure lest he spoil his young companion's evening. *Requiescat in pace.*" Urban meant to write a story along those lines.

He actually writes the story of a rather conceited, confident, crudely polished, energetic, designedly thoughtful, reluctantly obedient, determinedly chaste, and, amazingly, basically charitable human being. In an interview with Donald McDonald, published in *The Critic* for October–November, 1960, Powers calls Urban "a poor man's Fulton Sheen. . . . He's what

104 used to be called the Pullman type, now the type with the attache case, doing lots of good and instilling a feeling in the young men in the novitiate."

Urban does tool enthusiastically about in a borrowed Barracuda, using those about him for the ends he chooses to think are God's. But the story ends as written by God, it would seem, not by Urban, and in the final lines of the book the hill of St. Clement, so bitter an exile to the worldly priest, came to seem like home to the reborn Christian.

Powers's character is fully developed, and, like all truly profound literary characters, Urban makes his own choices—or seems to, at least. Hawthorne, in "The Custom-House," has indicated in classic fashion the way he as a literary artist approached his characters. While he was distracted by business affairs, his imagination was "a tarnished mirror," but when the conditions became ideal for meditation, for intuition, then some force "communicate[s], as it were, a heart and sensibilities of human tenderness to the forms which fancy summons up. It convert[s] them from snow-images into men and women."

Hawthorne is stating, if I read him correctly, that in such ideal conditions the characters act, or seem to act, on their own. They make, or seem to make, their own free, ultimate choices, as real men and women must. And even such ultimate free choices—the "yes" or "no" of which Hopkins speaks in "The Wreck of the Deutschland" and elsewhere—remain mysterious in real men and women, so also do they remain, or seem to, in true literary characters. The literary author, as Stephen Dedalus dimly grasped, does imitate God in creation. As God loves his human creatures enough to make them free, free enough to choose, if they will, their own destruction, so the literary artist loves and respects his own creation enough to leave it mysteriously free to choose (or seem to) its own destiny. In this mystery, I believe, Shakespeare's "whose worth's unknown" in Sonnet 116 finds its deepest meaning.

Powers creates Father Urban in this fashion, I judge. In speaking of Father Urban in the interview with Donald Mc-Donald, Powers said, "Father Urban was trying to develop something special for the Clementines. What it was, he was not sure—a kind of opportunism, I would say." Powers speaks as if Urban would have used some other term, would, in fact, have repudiated Powers's view. Father Urban, this remark suggests, has depths puzzling both to himself and to Powers. And certainly at the conclusion of the novel this mystery of the spirit's ultimate operation in relation to God, which Powers attempts to express mostly through indirection, looms above all the trivial clarities of daily routine.

Urban did choose his way of life, from his early choices under the influence of Msgr. Morez through Father Placidus and his choice of the Clementines to his preaching of retreats and parish missions. None of these, though, was a whole-hearted ultimate choice, since he still had a divided loyalty to God and to Mammon. Not until the golf ball hit him on the head and he set out on his final jousts, his final Pauline journeys, was he forced to his final "yes" or "no." And his ultimate "yes," spoken into infinity outside him, reaches our ears only as a mysterious silence—or, perhaps, as a faint reverberation emanating unexpectedly from the surprisingly ordinary acts of the new Provincial.

The hierarchy, seen largely through Urban's eyes, changes radically from the beginning to the end of the book. At the beginning, Placidus the athletic is the ideal, and Father Boniface the provincial is in imminent danger of joining "the select little group of people who'd made life unnecessarily difficult for Father Urban," a group to whom bad things happened. At the end, Father Urban resembles Boniface far more than he does Placidus. Like Sir Launcelot, he has died to that pragmatic and worldly self who set out so boldly to conquer the world on his own blatant and sufficient terms. He is no longer contemptuous of even the suddenly less obtuse Wilf.

106   The secular clergy, also seen through the faintly cynical eyes of the unregenerate Urban, reveals the weaknesses to which American priests are peculiarly liable—the prolonged and expensive vacations, the elegant cars, the resistance to change, the clerical politics. But the hard-working and self-sacrificing priests show up too, dedicating themselves without stint to the work of Christ and the service of others. Powers, like Joyce or Hawthorne, is concerned with expressing what he sees. He does not start with a doctrine and illustrate it, but builds on what he sees, and lets the consequences emerge as they will.

His treatment of the laity, seen once again largely through Urban's eyes, provides an interesting gallery. Billy Cosgrove, the rich, crude manipulator of humans, influences Urban profoundly. In order to get from Billy the wealth which will enable him to do the things "for Christ" that he plans, Urban compromises to the limit. To cooperate with Billy, he must assent to Billy's terms, which, it becomes increasingly evident, are not Christian ones. The limit finally comes when Billy attempts to drown a helpless deer in one of those lakes, as important to Urban as to Launcelot, where Urban's destiny works itself out. Urban's refusal to go along with Billy's act (he reads later that Teddy Roosevelt also condemned such conduct) loses Billy for him, but indicates the direction of Urban's ultimate choice.

Mrs. Thwaites, with her rejection of reality (two television sets in constant operation), her cruel and calculating perversion of piety (she could be compared to Joyce's Mrs. Mooney in "The Boarding House" on this point), her vicious treatment of her Irish maid, and her patronizing use of the priests, depicts the wealthy Catholic who wants, among other chattel, tame priests about the grounds. Father Urban once again, in his costly defense of the Irish maid, indicates the trend of his own will.

In Mr. Studley and Mr. Zimmerman, Powers contrasts the

worldly agnostic (or atheist) in operation, anxious to coexist with the Church if the terms can be found, and the pious fanatic who operates on the basis of ignorance and prejudice and fear, identifying God with his own warped notions of reality. Mr. Studley is the more interesting of the studies, and considerably more operative in Powers's structure, as I shall indicate in discussing his symbolic function.

Varied views of belief and love are widely operative in this novel, as in our society, and for my purposes here I shall examine three characters only—Jack, Sally, and Urban. Jack is a simple soul, childlike in his belief, wholehearted in his love. Intellectual he is not, though he is the one author the Clementines produce—at least the only one we observe in operation. In the opening chapter, "The Green Banana," he teaches Urban something about charity. Jack's dated pamphlet, "Danger Ahead," advocated teetotalism; however, thinking Urban wanted to do something friendly for him, Jack accepts Urban's invitation to the Pump Room, and, for Urban's sake, imbibes freely. Urban merely pretends "an excess of brotherly love" because he cannot bear to tell Jack that he too has been exiled to Minnesota. When Jack is overcome with the champagne, the basis at least is laid for Urban's understanding something of Jack's charity and Urban's excess of self-love. Urban does shake Jack awake "gently."

When they actually do meet at Deusterhaus, Jack once again makes the situation easy for Urban by stressing Urban's putative promise to pay them a visit, thus underplaying as much as he can Urban's original duplicity. When Urban gets into difficulty with Wilf over the bambino in the manger, Jack sacrifices his one secular passion, victory in checkers, in order to make Urban's unusual "conquest" a salve for the wound Wilf had inflicted.

Jack also writes, significantly, the knightly tales—"a *scholarly* children's edition of *Le Morte d'Arthur*"—which supply the immediate material for the title of the novel. These tales are no doubt like the books Jamesie and his aunt had read in "Jamesie"—"There they were, his old friends and hers—hers still. Perseus. Theseus. All those old Greeks. Sir Launcelot. Merlin. Sir Tristram. King Arthur. . . ." And Jack in this novel is much like the knight he himself esteemed most highly for belief and love, Sir Galahad.

Sally, shaky in her belief, knows that she is happier out of the Church than in. With her "fey quality"—like Morgan le Fay in more ways than one, and like a young animal who suddenly turns on her keeper—she tempts Urban with a profoundly attractive but false "love," which readily alters when it alteration finds. It is in his island experience with her, on an enchanted lake that is a microcosm, by a swan-bed woven of willow, that Urban experiences the call of the flesh. Like Eden, the island offers him a forbidden fruit, symbolized in the tiny red berries by the castle door, which "had tasted sweet and then bitter." Urban is again "unhorsed," literally unboated, into the lake, as he had been with Billy, and he has to swim for shore, sacrificing his shoes on the way. Since he had been hit on the head once more with one of Sally's shoes, and since he had meditated that "Life here below, no matter how much you might wish it otherwise, was shoes—not champagne, but shoes, and not dirt, but shoes, and this, roughly speaking, was the mind of the Church" (an image which might recall Hopkins's "Nor can foot feel, being shod"), the loss of Urban's shoes can readily be seen as his further sacrifice, in an increasingly final rejection of the things of this world, the shuffling off of the Old Man in favor of the New.

Urban himself is obviously the fullest portrayal of belief and of love that Powers has yet achieved. At the opening of the book, at the age of fifty-four, the securely confident Urban centers his interest in himself and judges the world outside by the reflection of it inside him. His efforts alone, he is convinced, can change things for the better. He stands solidly in his own shoes, and seeks the Grail of sanctity—as Marie J. Henault points out in a perceptive study of the Arthurian symbolism in the book (*America*, March 2, 1963)—in Pullman trains (first-class), in a red Barracuda S-X2, in a tan Rambler stationwagon. Then, as unfortunate events beyond his control break upon his unhelmeted head, like Lear, cornered, he changes. After the Bishop's golf ball hits him, he is time after time deprived of transportation, forced to swim in dangerous lakes, finally losing his own shoes and being forced to put on those of another priest. From the self-confident and critical operator of the opening, he becomes the quiet, humble, and kind priest of the epilogue. He has been, since he follows his barber's advice to stand on his head as a remedy for his headaches, literally as well as figuratively turned upside-down.

Sally has finally forced him to see himself as he really is: "I mean you're an operator—a trained operator like Mrs. Leeson, and an operator in your heart—and I don't think you have a friend in the world." As he endeavors to think of one friend, and cannot, he realizes that like those he most criticized, he has been using people. He sees himself in a detailed vision as he might have been had he chosen a business career—another crass and successful, spiritually dead and friendless Billy Cosgrove: "For many years I traveled out of Chicago, and I'm proud to call it my home. Expect from life? Only what any sane person would expect. What I've had from it. I've written my book, I've married my wife, I've made my pile. No complaints, no regrets. Who could ask for anything more?" From such a hell he retreats, and, having refused the temporal and temporary comfort Sally offers him, he returns to St. Clement's, where the illness of his soul is matched by the illness of his body, and, in knightly fashion, "he swoon[ed] dead away." He has almost reached the true goal of his travels, not in the way he intended to write the book of his life, but in the way God writes it—straight in crooked lines. He has come to perceive, as Didymus did in "Lions, Harts, Leaping Does," that the one way to reality is in simply looking outside. Thus, when Studley comes to visit in the final paragraphs, he is not treated as he was when he came to see Urban at St. Clement's

110   —when Urban told Wilf, "I don't really know him"; the new Urban, Father Provincial now, looking in love outside, sees to it that Studley enjoys "a wonderful couple of hours."

Powers's techniques in this novel excel the achievements of his short stories. The varied rhythms of his sentences express poetically a great deal more than the mere signification of the words making them. As one example, Urban, emerging from the lake shoeless after his sad adventure with Sally and his meditation on the necessity of shoes, symbols of human existence, is thus effectively described: "Wet and woebegone and shivering, he sat on a fallen birch and put on his socks and hid the whiteness of his feet from himself." The structure of the sentence follows carefully Urban's motions, the crowded adjectives his shaking, the successive clauses his two physical acts and one symbolic act, the last longer and more weighted with meaning than the others. Those pale and delicate feet not only recall to him in Freudian context the glowing flesh of Sally but remind him of his own inadequacy to walk barefoot painfully to the hill which is not yet home to him.

The principal symbols Powers finds in his material are drawn from Pauline and Arthurian backgrounds. Like Joyce, Powers, coming to his material with a passionately imagined point of view, does not impose symbols but finds them. Conceiving of Urban as a successor of the apostles sent by Christ (certainly Urban's view of himself), he sees him in his early years as a Saul—worldly rather than Christian, persecuting rather than aiding the members of Christ's body. That is perhaps too strong a condemnation of Urban's activity before his being struck down by Christ and converted, but something of it appears in the implied comparisons between Urban and St. Paul. The beginning of Paul's conversion is described in Acts, 9:1–10:

During his journey, it happened, as he was approaching Damascus, that suddenly a light from the sky flashed round about him, and falling to the ground, he heard a voice saying to him, "Saul, Saul, why do you persecute me?" "Who are you, Lord?" he asked. Jesus replied, "I am Jesus whom you are persecuting. Arise and go into the city, and you will be told what you must do." Meanwhile his traveling companions remained speechless. They heard the voice but saw no one. Then Saul arose from the ground, and although his eyes were open, he could see nothing. So leading him by the hand, they brought him into Damascus. For three whole days he could not see, neither did he eat or drink.

This experience is referred to in the chapter "God Writes . . ." in relation to Mr. Thwaites: "Andrew had been a great enemy of the Church, like St. Paul, but there had been no road to Damascus for Andrew." There had been just such a road for Urban, when Christ through his vicar had struck down Urban, who, like Paul, was blinded for three days. During this time, lying in his hospital bed, Urban "listening with the ears of one blind, wondered greatly at the ways of men." Then, again like Paul, he goes on three missionary journeys, to Mrs. Thwaites' to rescue "a damsel in distress," to the north with Billy to Henn's Haven, to Belleisle with Sally. In each journey he suffered some of Paul's perils and defeats—"Once I was stoned, three times I suffered shipwreck; a night and a day I was adrift on the high sea; in frequent journeys on foot . . ." (2 Corinthians, 11)—and at the end of the last trip he is greeted by Msgr. Renton with that prelate's not insignificant favorite expletive: "Holy Paul!" Imprisoned finally like Paul in the Provincial's office, from which his letters go out to the people of God, concealing his suffering and infirmity from others, he offers like Paul his aching head to the Lord he serves.

The ubiquitous Arthurian symbolism emerges most clearly in such chapters as "Wrens and Starlings," in which the golf game is conceived in terms of a knightly joust, and in "Belleisle," in which the play castle of Sally recalls the legends of Guinevere and the Elaines. Again like Joyce, Powers does not draw up any consistent mathematical relationships of character to prototype, but lets the situation dictate the analogies. Urban is at one point explicitly allied to Lancelot (or Sir Launcelot, as Jack prefers). Jack wrote: "There Sir Launcelot died to the world. . . . The noblest knight of the world [took] such abstinence that he waxed full lean." "You've lost some weight," Urban's barber informs him in the next sentence. Powers thus invites us to see Urban throughout as the noble Lancelot, so apparently successful yet so faulty in his earlier years, achieving the life of the spirit through death to the world only in his final retirement to the hermitage— —where home was not Camelot (or Chicago), but the bleak hill, on which Pauline crucifixion of the materialism and sensuality of the world ties together the Arthurian and Christian themes.

A more detailed examination of one of the minor figures in Powers's symbolic structure may throw more light on the intricate patterning of the narrative. Mr. Studley shows up first in "Twenty-four Hours in a Strange Diocese," in which he is neighbor to but disliked by the fanatically right-wing Zimmermans. He smells of beer and is fascinated by the golf course at St. Clements, but even more by the airstrip he imagines to be there (recall that Father Burner, the Prince of Darkness, took flying lessons). He will not call Urban "Father," quoting Scripture ineptly to justify this rude slight. He notes the absence of Urban's Roman collar (which, Urban tells Sally later, he is always losing). Studley is deeply interested in the worldly red Barracuda, as is his smelly dog, Frank. Frank, joining Studley in trying out the car, sits on Urban's priestly garb, and later curls up on top of Urban's coat. Both Studley and Frank "looked right at home in the car," which, by the way, had earlier seemed to Urban not "right for him." Studley offers alcohol to Urban, thus tempting him to his place and to a view of his plane, "a World War I four-winged machine, bright red, with a number of heraldic devices painted on it: dice which had come up seven; the ace of spades;

the leg of a female, ending in a high-heeled shoe; and a
mustachioed man in a high silk hat on the band of which appeared the words 'Sir Satan.' " Grover Studley, whose name
suggests a businesslike attitude toward sensuality, thus becomes ever more clearly a symbol of America's Prince of Darkness, or at least of Urban's demon, a figure from the heady
twenties. Studley is retired, since he doesn't have much to do
in our materialistic civilization, but he indicates instant
readiness to get back to work in his plane if need arises. He
puts on goggles and sits in the plane. "Seems a long time ago,"
he says (no doubt in the groves of Eden). He insists that Urban
sit in his plane, since he had sat in Urban's borrowed vehicle.
When Urban crawls into the rear cockpit, which smells
strongly of Frank, Frank growls, as if to indicate that a priest
does not belong there. Mr. Studley, "when he touched down,"
insists that Urban sign his guest book, crowded with priests'
names, not all met at Zimmerman's. Studley's favorite expletive is "hell," and the word is juxtaposed to "sky," which
threatens thunder. Studley's presence slows but does not stop
discussion of the day's gospel, Luke 16:1–9, on the unjust
steward. The text was used previously at the end of the "Over-
ture" which began the book, when Urban was described as acting like the steward. (This is, by the way, the text Joyce uses
for Father Purdon's venal sermon in "Grace.") Studley defends
the steward, claiming that "unjust" merely means "inac-
curate," a pretty close approximation of Father Purdon's approach. Urban is uncomfortable with Studley's assumption of
intimate friendship and of agreement between them. The
party is broken up by "a tremendous clap of thunder" which
alarms Studley, who flees.

The symbolism of Studley as American devil-figure works
effectively and without strain, since Powers lets the realistic
level of his narrative control and contain the symbolic level.
He does not drop the symbol here, but uses it to good point in
unifying the book. In Urban's vision of himself as worldly

business man in "Belleisle," Studley appears. Like Mr. Kernan in Joyce's "Grace," Urban conceives of himself as briskly and deliberately unfaithful: "He had got away, he hadn't fallen away, from the faith of his fathers. Was that *Andrew Thwaites*, Mr. Studley? Indeed it was, son, and he likes your style. He could do a lot for you. There's just one thing. . . ." Mr. Studley is here the tempting devil, who, having succeeded with Andrew Thwaites, who lacked a road to Damascus, offers to Urban, as he did to Christ in the Temptation, worldly riches and power for the price of the one thing necessary. That "one thing" to be sacrificed will be Urban's belief and love, "if, falling down, you will adore me."

Thus Mr. Studley's visit on the final page of the novel takes on new and profound meaning, and his repeated announcement of Frank's death echoes the death of something undesirable and hellish in Urban. Frank's death, by the way, is balanced in the second-last paragraph of the book with the news of the health of Rex, Wilfred's helpful and friendly dog.

Urban as a real Christian is no more a socially effective man than he was before his conversion. In his pre-conversion dealings with Billy Cosgrove, for example, he did not at any time achieve communication. He had to subordinate himself to Billy's godless terms. He cannot communicate with Billy after his conversion either, as another godly man might well have been able to do. He is not an effective provincial, though he has become a sincerely Christian man. Nor would he have been an effective provincial before his conversion, as Placidus was not. Powers shows us in Urban not the ideal operative Christian, but this particular limited Christian. The god of his civilization prevented him from looking outside, and obscured, until his ultimate and humble "yes," the God of Christianity.

Powers's symbolism, then, does a great deal to unify and deepen the expression of his vision of reality. If Granville Hicks and others who share his opinion were to read *Morte d'Urban* as a profoundly symbolic novel, like *A Portrait of the*

Artist as a Young Man or *Ulysses*, they would be less likely to say, as Mr. Hicks does in *The Saturday Review of Literature* for May 20, 1967, that "the novel, I thought, fell apart." Powers's ending does, at first sight, look bleak and motionless after the bustle and hilarity which precede it, but when the symbolic resonances sound in the spirit their "ditties of no tone," the depth and complexity of Powers's vision of our American Vanity Fair and the goal of the book's constant drive through human love toward divine love become more apparent, teasing us out of thought as does the mystery of eternity.

NOTES

1. This essay was in print before I saw John V. Hagopian's excellent book, *J. F. Powers* (New York: Twayne, 1968). Mr. Hagopian's discussion of the pastor of Father Fabre's parish (pp. 99–105) has nearly persuaded me that I am naive and mistaken in my view of the pastor as Christ-like. Mr. Hagopian holds that the astute reader will notice that the change occurs in Father Fabre, not in the pastor, who throughout simply rejects all that he finds difficult or embarrassing. But the text, as I read it, leaves open the possibility that Father Fabre's more kindly judgment of the pastor may be rooted in an operative if primitive charity in the old man. There is, surely, some charity in his giving up the chair to his curate in "A Losing Game." Still, Mr. Hagopian's view, I suspect, better reveals Power's intention than does mine.

6

Harry J. Mooney, Jr.

Moments of Eternity:
A Study in the Short Stories
of Flannery O'Connor

Because her art to some extent depended upon its pre-
ternatural intensity, Flannery O'Connor appears at her best
and most characteristic in her short stories. Moreover, in the
best of them she developed, over the fairly brief years of her
creative life, the themes that challenged her deeply, the values
in which she most believed, and the unique moral and religious
vision which defines every line she ever wrote. To examine
them with some care is to arrive at a firmer appreciation of her
qualities as an artist of a completely original kind.

I

Eschatology casts its long shadow across all of Flannery
O'Connor's stories. For this reason, the confrontation between
good and evil which they represent is usually stark, yet it is
also subtle and capable of all sorts of ironic reversals. One of
the primary sources of evil in these stories arises from persons
so self-sufficient or, in terms of the stories themselves, so
limited, that they either reject or deny God because they can-

not conceive the need of anything outside themselves. In "A Good Man Is Hard to Find," the Misfit appears to belong, in an especially terrifying way, to just this category: to the grandmother's exhortation that he pray for help, the Misfit replies, " 'I don't want no help. I'm doing all right by myself.' " At the conclusion of the story, however, he states the meaning of the life, death, and resurrection of Christ in absolute terms. He perceives in Christ's appearance on earth a truth so radical that it alters the very nature of human life; yet he cannot be sure whether it *is* truth:

"Jesus was the only one that ever raised the dead," the Misfit continued, "and He shouldn't have done it. He thrown everything off balance. If he did what He said, then it's nothing for you to do but throw everything away and follow him, and if He didn't, then it's nothing for you to do but enjoy the few minutes you got left the best way you can—by killing someone or burning down his house or doing some other meanness to him. No pleasure but meanness," he said and his voice had become almost a snarl.

Since the Misfit is just about to shoot the grandmother he appears to have chosen the second alternative, and indeed he has already disposed of her family. Yet just before he fires at her he laments not having been alive during the time of Christ: " 'It ain't right I wasn't there because if I had been there I would have known.' " The Misfit is terrifying, then, because his rejection is firmly based on the possibility of belief; in fact he sees a world penetrated by Christ—" 'He thrown everything off balance' "—and he understands Christ's life as a demand for a total transformation of human existence.

There is another delusion of self-sufficiency, deriving from the power of property, which constitutes the central concern of other Flannery O'Connor stories. Through property, in stories like "A Circle in the Fire" and "A View of the Woods," a character hopes to achieve a kind of independence or even permanence; yet he is doomed to a horrible defeat partly be-

cause property also represents a constriction, and ultimately
a denial, of the true freedom of the person. Mrs. Cope, in "A
Circle in the Fire," cannot escape a feeling of oppression in
relation to her land: "She looked around at her rich pastures
and hills heavy with timber and shook her head as if it might
all be a burden she was trying to shake off her back." When
Powell appears with his companions, he is a threat to everything in which Mrs. Cope believes, and she herself immediately perceives the nature of that threat: "Powell sat down on
the edge of one of the chairs and looked as if he were trying to
enclose the whole place in one encircling stare." Private realms
of property are in fact an absurdity, and Powell represents a
kind of ruthless public invasion of such a tenuous realm. They
are also a kind of attempt to escape God, and the evil of the
three boys' arson is on another level a clarification, as well as
a confirmation, of Mrs. Cope's obsessive fear. The irony is
made clear in one line when one of the boys in the moment
just before the fire is set says, " 'Man, Gawd owns them woods
and her too.' " And the fire then begins to burn in an enclos-
ing circle, like justice and truth and the swift descent of God
into the world of man. In the final simile of the story the boys
are likened to "the prophets . . . dancing in the fiery furnace,
in the circle the angel had cleared for them."

The relationship of the grandfather to his granddaughter
in "A View of the Woods" illustrates a principle comparable
to that at the center of "A Circle in the Fire." In the child the
old man sees the same acquisitive drive that is his own central
characteristic; all the rest of his family he holds in contempt,
threatening them by selling off pieces of his property. In his
property he beholds an autonomy for himself, an autonomy
which he expresses in terms of that power over others which
it seems to give him. But this autonomy is in turn threatened:
the old man is governed by the fear that the child may in
actuality resemble her father rather than himself. In the terrible fight between the girl and the grandfather which con-

cludes the story, the girl indeed asserts her identity in relation to her father. "The old man looked up into his image. It was triumphant and hostile. 'You been whipped,' it said, 'by me,' and then it added, 'and I'm PURE Pitts.'" The grandfather now recognizes that he has turned on "the face that was his own but dared to call itself Pitts." Killing the girl, he asserts desperately, "'There's not an ounce of Pitts in me,'" thus revealing his knowledge both that he cannot insure his autonomy through the child and that the Pitts streak embodies a number of forces, both within and without himself, which he fears. At the end of the story, the grandfather lies on the ground, trapped in the center of his own land.

A third kind of individual occurring regularly in Flannery O'Connor's stories is the righteous, but the sources of righteousness are multiple. In its simplest, but nevertheless highly destructive, form, this quality is represented by Thomas in "The Comforts of Home." Thomas believes both in virtue and in the devil, but he has no perception of complexity. When he suddenly confronts it he acts badly and unwittingly creates a situation in which only the violent and irrational prevail. Thomas's righteousness, then, is a lack of knowledge, a kind of unawareness; furthermore, it is in essence a lack of religious awareness, for it oversimplifies the contest between good and evil by insisting upon absolutes.

Far more profound diagnoses of righteousness are conducted in "Revelation" and "The Displaced Person," each among Flannery O'Connor's finest stories. In the first Mrs. Turpin has her own secure sense of God's people:

Sometimes Mrs. Turpin occupied herself at night naming the classes of people. On the bottom of the heap were most colored people, not the kind she would have been if she had been one, but most of them; then next to them—not above, just away from— were the white trash; then above them were the homeowners, and above them the home-and-land owners, to which she and Claud belonged. Above she and Claud were people with a

lot of money and bigger houses and much more land. But here
the complexity of it would begin to bear in on her, for some
of the people with a lot of money were common and ought to
be below she and Claud and some of the people who had good blood
had lost their money and had to rent and then there were
colored people who owned their homes and land as well. There
was a colored dentist in town who had two red Lincolns and a
swimming pool and a farm with registered whiteface cattle on it.
Usually by the time she had fallen asleep all the classes of
people were moiling and roiling around in her head, and she would
dream they were all crammed in together in a box car, being
ridden off to be put in a gas oven.

In contrast to Thomas in "The Comforts of Home," Mrs.
Turpin is guilty of a far more presumptuous error: whereas
he misunderstands good and evil by reductive oversimplification, she regards both man and creation as if these were her
own. Nevertheless she dimly perceives, though she cannot
appreciate its significance, some relationship between her own
pyramidal vision and gas ovens. Yet she is a woman who feels
extreme gratitude to God, so deeply does she appreciate her
superiority to others:

To help anybody out that needed it was her philosophy of life.
She never spared herself when she found somebody in need,
whether they were white or black, trash or decent. And of all
she had to be thankful for, she was most thankful that this was so.
If Jesus had said, "You can be high society and have all the
money you want and be thin and svelte, but you can't be a good
woman with it," she would have to say, "Well don't make me
that then. Make me a good woman and it don't matter what else,
how fat or how ugly or how poor!" Her heart rose. He had not
made her a nigger or white trash or ugly! He had made her
herself and given her a little bit of everything. Jesus, thank you!
she said. Thank you thank you thank you! Whenever she
counted her blessings she felt as bouyant as if she weighed
one hundred and twenty-five pounds instead of one hundred
and eighty.

122 When the young girl in the doctor's waiting-room says to her, " 'Go back to hell where you came from, you old wart hog,' " Mrs. Turpin is amazed by much more than the abruptness and impoliteness of the statement: she instantly perceives that "there was trash in the room to whom it might justly have been applied." Toward the end of the story, just before her final vision of a translation of souls in which she occupies a subordinate position, and while she is studying the hogs on the farm to determine the meaning of the message sent to her through the girl, Mrs. Turpin finds all her customary assumptions overturned. She has a shattering sense that God's order may be far more complex and inclusive than her own: " 'If you like trash better, go get yourself some trash then. You could have made me trash. Or a nigger. If trash is what you wanted, why didn't you make me trash?' "

Righteousness is the sponsor of prejudice, a fact emphasized in "The Displaced Person," the long story in many ways central to Flannery O'Connor's total achievement. Unlike the shorter stories, "The Displaced Person" develops in two sections, with the focus falling on Mrs. Shortley in the first and Mrs. McIntyre in the second. Although Mrs. Shortley had once seen in a newsreel a heap of naked, dead bodies, victims of the brutality and evil of the war, this picture had had no real meaning for her except as it signified the inferiority of other persons and places: "That was the kind of thing that was happening every day in Europe where they had not advanced as in this country. . . ." And when she sees the priest who brings the Guizac family, the displaced persons, to the farm, Mrs. Shortley remembers that these people did not have "an advanced religion." She also reveals her blindness to the splendor and transcendence of God's order, to the way in which temporal reality is penetrated and shaped by eternal truth. (Because righteousness is a blindness, a contraction of the complexity of creation, those who suffer from it fail, in more ways than one, to recognize God as he manifests himself in the world.) When the priest beholds on the farm a peacock with spread tail, he cries, " 'So beautiful,' " and Mrs. Shortley responds merely, " 'Nothing but a peachicken.' " Her exclusiveness, her prejudice and her lack of vision coalesce at another point when, facing the blaze of the peacock's tail, she sees in it only a series of displaced persons invading and taking over all of America. Ironically, however, and therefore appropriately, Mrs. Shortley discovers herself a displaced person by her own unwitting design, and dies of the shock of the discovery. More and more driven by the presence of the Guizacs, by the plot which they and the priest must have hatched to displace those already secure, Mrs. Shortley cries to God to be delivered from "the stinking power of Satan."

And she started from that day to read her Bible with a new attention. She poured over the Apocalypse and began to quote from the Prophets and before long she had come to a deeper understanding of her existence. She saw plainly that the meaning of the world was a mystery that had been planned and she was not surprised that she had a special part in the plan because she was strong. She saw that the Lord God Almighty had created the strong people to do what had to be done and she felt that she would be ready when she was called. Right now she felt that her business was to watch the priest.

The mystery of God's providence, then, is not really a mystery to Mrs. Shortley: she too clearly sees her own role in asserting, and thus contracting, it. In her prophecy, " 'The children of wicked nations will be butchered,' " Mrs. Shortley unconsciously reveals the way in which her simple-minded separation of the good from the evil contributes to those newsreel pictures the relevance which, to persons like herself, she had automatically denied.

In the second part of the story, Mrs. McIntyre, who unites the power of property and the assertiveness it arouses with her own kind of righteousness, separates herself completely from the kind of suffering represented by the Guizacs: she has no responsibility for it, she believes, and in so declaring reveals herself as blind to the vision embodied in the peacock as well. After rejecting any possibility of involvement in the condition of the Guizacs, Mrs. McIntyre broadens the point: " 'I'm not responsible for the world's misery,' " she says, and the statement has a double edge of harshness and insensitivity because it is delivered to Mr. Guizac himself. When the priest visits her, Mrs. McIntyre explains, " 'Listen! I'm not theological. I'm practical. I want to talk to you about something practical.' " The connection between these assertions and her blindness (she shares this quality of course with Mrs. Shortley) to the peacock is very precisely developed. If she cannot understand the community of suffering, neither can she understand the real meaning of the Incarnation and Redemption, and the peacock is the symbol of the radical transformation in reality worked by Christ.

The priest let his eyes wander towards the birds. They had reached the middle of the lawn. The cock stopped suddenly and curving his neck backwards, he raised his tail and spread it with a shimmering timbrous noise. Tiers of small pregnant suns floated in a green-gold haze over his head. The priest stood transfixed, his jaw slack. "Christ will come like that!" he said in a loud gay voice and wiped his hand over his mouth and stood there, gaping.

Mrs. McIntyre's face assumed a set puritanical expression and she reddened. Christ in a conversation embarrassed her the way sex had her mother. "It is not my responsibility that Mr. Guizac has nowhere to go," she said. "I don't find myself responsible for all the extra people in the world."

The old man didn't seem to hear her. His attention was fixed on the cock who was taking minute steps backward, his head against the spread tail. "The Transfiguration," he murmured.

She had no idea what he was talking about. "Mrs. Guizac didn't have to come here in the first place," she said, giving him a hard look.

The cock lowered his tail and began to pick grass.

"He didn't have to come in the first place," she repeated, emphasizing each word.

The old man smiled absently. "He came to redeem us," he said and blandly reached for her hand and shook it and said he must go.

Mrs. McIntyre's inability to distinguish in this conversation between Christ and Mr. Guizac is ironically echoed a little later when she says to the priest, "As far as I'm concerned, Christ was just another D.P." An important key to the quality of Flannery O'Connor's irony is provided here, for it is Mrs. McIntyre, stating the nature of her separation from suffering and from Mr. Guizac and from Christ, who makes the central point of the story: that Christ *is* Mr. Guizac, and therefore another D.P. Mrs. McIntyre's blindness to all of this exacts a terrible toll: ultimately, goaded by a sense of her property and, like Mrs. Shortley, of her own ironic displacement, she becomes an accomplice to Mr. Shortley in the death of Mr. Guizac. Following that death, Mrs. McIntyre finds herself in a new territory. Like Mrs. Shortley, suddenly perceiving at the end of the story's first section "the tremendous frontiers of her true country," Mrs. McIntyre discovers herself, just at the moment when Mr. Guizac becomes a corpse, in "some foreign country where the people bent over the body were natives. . . ." From this vision she never recovers, but she is of course transformed in a way quite different from that announced by the peacock. Nevertheless those qualities which the priest perceived in the peacock and which she steadfastly renounced have proved themselves, in her desolation, the fundamental components not simply of a religious vision but of reality itself.

II

A number of Flannery O'Connor's characters, then, inhabit a withered landscape because they are blind to the

126 existence of, and their own need for, grace; but their self-dependence is of course delusive. This is why their lives are often shattered by revelations of an order beyond their grasp, revelations from which many of them seem unlikely ever to recover. As if to illustrate this theme, many of these stories develop the concept of a journey, some briefly and lightly, some far more fundamentally. In "A Good Man Is Hard to Find," the grandmother checks the mileage as she and her family leave Atlanta "because she thought it would be interesting to see how many miles they had been when they got back." During the car trip, the old woman seems to inhabit two areas of existence at the same time, for just before the concussion of the accident projects her into the world of the Misfit, she remembers that the house from her past for which she has been searching is not in Georgia after all. (In several important respects, however, this story is not characteristic of the pattern under investigation: the Misfit, with his perception that Christ has " 'thrown everything off balance,' " makes a powerful statement of Christ's primacy, and under circumstances which create a devastating irony, but the grandmother cannot be said to suffer from any blindness of the kind embodied in the women of "The Displaced Person.")

The boy Harry Ashfield, in "The River," moves from the narrow world of his mother's apartment to that of Mrs. Connin and the evangelist, Bevel, from whom he learns that he derives from Jesus Christ and not merely from a doctor, as he has been taught. The profundity of the change which this encounter works in the boy is suggested by the fact that even *before* it occurs the boy has taken the name of Bevel for himself. Indeed two worlds collide in the boy's mind following the actual Bevel's disclosure:

He had found out already this morning that he had been made by a carpenter named Jesus Christ. Before he had thought it had been a doctor named Sladewell, a fat man with a yellow mustache who gave him shots and thought his name was Herbert, but this must have been a joke. They joked a lot where he lived. If he had thought about it before, he would have thought Jesus was a word like "oh" or "dam" or "God," or maybe somebody who had cheated them out of something sometime. When he had asked Mrs. Connin who the man in the sheet over the bed was, she had looked at him a while with her mouth open. Then she had said, "That's Jesus," and she had kept on looking at him.

The recurrent journey theme occurs as the boy enters the woods on his way to the river and the evangelist: "He had never been in woods before and he walked carefully, looking from side to side as if he were entering a strange country." The division between his old country and his new he perceives in terms of the seriousness of the latter: held by the evangelist, the boy perceives that "this was not a joke," whereas "where he lived everything was a joke." The boy's journey is absolute, for it is impossible for him, in any genuine sense, to return to the world of his mother's apartment, and his mother's behavior towards him after his encounter with the evangelist merely leads to his increased awareness that this part of his life has ended: "Then he left the apartment and caught the car at the corner. He hadn't taken a suitcase because there was nothing from there he wanted to keep."

But there is a further division in "The River" still remaining to be resolved—that which appears in the figure of Mr. Paradise who, in Mrs. Connin's words, " 'always comes to show he ain't been healed.' " Seeing Bevel return to the river, Mr. Paradise takes candy and begins to follow the boy, as if to enter into contest with the power of the water and the evangelist. The conclusion of "The River" is doubly ironic, enveloping in brief strokes both the boy and Mr. Paradise. The former, seeking in the water the Kingdom of Christ, the final stage of his journey, is in a sense delivered into it by Mr. Paradise's pursuit, for when he first puts his head beneath the water and pushes forward it seems to him that the water will not have him:

> He thought how far he had come for nothing and he began to hit and kick and splash the filthy river. His feet were already treading on nothing. Then he heard a shout and turned his head and saw something like a giant pig bounding after him, shaking a red and white club and shouting. He plunged under once and this time, the waiting current caught him like a long gentle hand and pulled him swiftly forward and down. For an instant he was overcome with surprise; then since he was moving quickly and knew that he was getting somewhere, his fury and fear left him.
>
> Mr. Paradise's head appeared from time to time on the surface of the water. Finally, far downstream, the old man rose like some ancient water monster and stood empty-handed, staring with his dull eyes as far down the river line as he could see.

Mr. Paradise's desolation, though particularized according to his circumstances, is characteristic of those confronted suddenly by an order which restricted and necessarily temporal values cannot explain.

The thematic concept of a journey is related merely to a staircase in "A Stroke of Good Fortune," for the ascent of these stairs seems beyond the power of the sick and dizzy Ruby. By the time she *has* mounted them, however, she possesses a knowledge of herself which constitutes a kind of journey into another county. In "The Artificial Nigger," on the other hand, the metaphor is far more extended. Mr. Head, feeling perfectly in command of his physical and moral reactions, wears an expression of wisdom which seems to entitle him to function as one of the great guides of men: "He might have been Vergil summoned in the middle of the night to go to Dante, or better, Raphael, awakened by a blast of God's light to fly to the side of Tobias." On that trip to the city which the story describes, Mr. Head, although he has been here only twice before, acts, in the beginning at least, as his grandson's guide.

Living in a country that has banished all its Negroes more than a decade earlier, Mr. Head naturally identifies the city with Negroes and with the possibility of his son's seeing one for the first time. In his role as cicerone he describes the sewerage system so vividly that his grandson "connected the sewer passages with the entrance to hell and understood for the first time how the world was put together in its lower parts." But even as the old man appears to be guiding a course, Nelson perceives that they are really moving in a circle. When the boy stops an older Negro woman to ask help in finding their way out of the maze, he knows that she is making fun of him, yet "he suddenly wanted her to reach down and pick him up and draw him against her and then he wanted to feel her breath on his face. He wanted to look down and down into her eyes while she held him tighter and tighter. He had never had such a feeling before. He felt as if he were reeling down through a pitch-black tunnel." Nelson feels such a sensation because, like many other characters in Flannery O'Connor's world, he has lived with such narrow assumptions that the unexpected shatters him. Consequently he is ashamed and takes the old man's hand, revealing a dependence he usually tries to reject. If the boy thus betrays his feeling for the Negro woman, however, Mr. Head betrays the boy himself when, after he has overturned a garbage can and upset an elderly woman, the police come. The grandfather says merely: " 'This is not my boy. I never seen him before.' " Towards the end of the story Mr. Head no longer feels like a guide, for his moral desolation transforms the haunted urban circle he traverses: "He knew that now he was wandering into a strange black place where nothing was like it had ever been before, a long old age without respect and an end that would be welcome because it would be the end." On his way with Nelson to a suburban train stop to which he has finally been directed, Mr. Head suddenly knows "what man would be like without salvation." But this journey into desolation ends in a revelation, through the old man's discovery of a strange plaster cast of a Negro, of an entirely different quality. Mr. Head now experiences in a flash what earlier that same day he would have been incapable of knowing: the simultaneous sense of his own weaknesses and the overwhelming love and mercy of God:

> He stood appalled, judging himself with the thoroughness of God, while the action of mercy covered his pride like a flame and consumed it. He had never thought himself a great sinner before but he saw now that his true depravity had been hidden from him lest it cause him despair. He realized that he was forgiven from sins from the beginning of time, when he had conceived in his own heart the sin of Adam, until the present, when he had denied poor Nelson. He saw that no sin was too monstrous for him to claim as his own, and since God loved in proportion as He forgave, he felt ready at that instant to enter Paradise.

Thus a journey which has contracted into a circle as restricted and haunting as that of "A Circle in the Fire," suddenly expands to include eternity in Mr. Head's swift knowledge of God's love and mercy.

Sometimes the theme of the journey is expressed only indirectly; in "Parker's Back," as in "The River," it is worked out in terms of identity. The protagonist's half-rejected awareness of other realms than the secular is clearly indicated at the beginning of the story: "Long views depressed Parker. You look out into space like that and you begin to feel as if someone were after you, the navy or the government or religion." After his apocalypse, when his tractor overturns with him beneath a sun that has the appearance of eternity, Parker selects for the tattoo on the long-reserved space on his back a Byzantine face of Christ "with all-demanding eyes." Yet when the artist questions him concerning religion, Parker makes a denial of a kind which might issue from many persons in these stories: " 'Naw, I ain't got no use for none of that. A man can't save his self from whatever it is he don't deserve none of my sympathy.' " But Parker cannot escape the eyes of the face on his back: "He felt as though under their gaze, he was as transparent as the wing of a fly." And the words of his denial are contradicted in a way which he cannot quite understand: "These words seemed to leave his mouth like wraiths and to evaporate at once as if he had never uttered them." In one of the most intensely ironic scenes in all of Flannery O'Connor's stories, Parker enters a pool hall and, pentecostally, brings the Holy Spirit into the midst of its uncomprehending habitues. A fight breaks out, "like a whirlwind on a summer's day," and Parker, ejected, examines his soul, discovers all his past lies, and knows that he must now follow the eyes on his back. "It was as if he were himself but a stranger to himself, driving into a new country though everything he saw was familiar to him, even at night." Having earlier denied his real name, Obadiah, just as he had denied his interest in religion, he is now forced to call himself by this name before his wife will admit him to his house. There is, however, a final irony: his wife chases him out again because she is horrified by the " 'idolatry' " of the tattooed Christ. The story concludes from her point of view, but by establishing once again O. E. Parker's new identity: "She looked toward the pecan tree and her eyes hardened still more. There he was —who called himself Obadiah Elihue—leaning against the tree, crying like a baby."

III

A reversal of an often savage kind operates in many of Flannery O'Connor's stories, but it is a reversal which usually illustrates the development of a natural law. Again it is the righteous and the reductive who most frequently fall victim to it. In "Good Country People," the agnostic Joy has reduced life and the world to her own kind of intelligibility; once she cries out to her mother, " 'Woman! do you ever look inside? Do you ever look inside and see what you are *not*? God!

132 Malebranche was right: we are not our own light. We are not
our own light!' " But darkness, it turns out, can be robbed by
darkness, and the agonistic thus deprived of her faith. The
young Bible salesman who takes her artificial leg from her
speaks as if he were depriving her of her soul: " 'It's what
makes you different. You ain't like anybody else.' " But the
terrible moment of illumination, and the appropriate irony
around which the story is constructed, occur when Joy re-
proaches the young man for not acting like a Christian, like
the Bible salesman he purports to be, and hears, unbelievingly,
his reply: " 'I hope you don't think,' he said in a lofty tone,
'that I believe in that crap! I may sell Bibles but I know which
end is up and I wasn't born yesterday and I know where I'm
going.' "

Mr. Shiftlet, in "The Life You Save May Be Your Own,"
prophesies doom as if this were his natural function, for he
perceives all the evil of the world. " 'Nothing is like it used to
be, lady,' " he tells Mrs. Crater, " 'The world is almost
rotten.' " Although he particularly protests any excessive
attachment to the material, he is himself vulnerable: when he
finishes resuscitating the old Crater car which is the object of
his own avaricious dream, "he had an expression of serious
modesty on his face as if he had just raised the dead." When
in conversation he wishes to draw a distinction between body
and spirit, he compares the spirit to an automobile (" 'But the
spirit, lady, is always on the move, always . . .' ") in order to
clarify its nature for Mrs. Crater. Finally, when Mr. Shiftlet
has married and abandoned Mrs. Crater's daughter in order
to acquire the car, he suddenly finds himself being borne in it
towards some fierce storm of an apocalyptic order. Nevertheless he does manage to some extent to keep his own values and
reductions intact: if the storm embodies all that rottenness in
the world which he has so clearly known, and if it threatens to
engulf *him* too, he can only pray that he may be delivered
from it, thus preserving his own righteousness, his self-

justification: "Mr. Shiftlet felt that the rottenness of the world was about to engulf him. He raised his arm and let it fall again to his breast. 'Oh, Lord,' he prayed, 'Break forth and wash the slime from this earth!' "

Perhaps no single story treats so compellingly the laws called into operation by the righteous as "The Lame Shall Enter First." When Sheppard, a City Recreational Director, faces at a reformatory a fourteen-year-old boy, Rufus Johnson, who has no hesitation in attributing his own bad behavior to Satan, saying, " 'He has me in his power,' " he replies automatically, " 'Rubbish! We're living in the space age! You're too smart to give me an answer like that!' " Sheppard of course does not merely reject the supernatural; he attempts to replace it by the order of the rationally explicable. But his righteousness, even according to the norm suggested by some of the other stories, is unbearable: " 'If I can help a person, all I want is to do it. I'm above and beyond simple pettiness,' " he says of himself. But Rufus says of him to his son, " 'God, kid, how do you stand it? He thinks he's Jesus Christ!' "

Sheppard's assured denial of religion, especially in its eschatological aspect, exacts a terrible price in his own natural world. When his son Norton asks where his dead mother has gone, the father can only answer, " 'Your mother isn't anywhere. She's not unhappy. She just isn't.' " After all, he thinks of himself and the boy, "he could not allow himself to bring him up on a lie." But just at the moment when Sheppard denies any concept of immortality, the same Rufus who has defined himself as acting under Satan's power asks whether the dead woman believed in Jesus; learning that she did, he describes her as saved and now " 'on high.' " In his concern for Rufus, Sheppard has constantly neglected his own son; now he is determined that if Rufus is merely trying to annoy him by projecting religious belief into the boy, he will refuse to be irritated, for "Norton was not bright enough to be damaged much," and "Heaven and hell were for the mediocre, and he was that if he was anything." As a result of Rufus's words to Norton, however, the telescope Sheppard has bought in the hope of inculcating in the boys a sense of the modern age of science and astronauts and religious disbelief becomes the instrument by which his son studies the heavens where he now believes his dead mother to be.

Sheppard's relationship to Rufus is certainly no easier than his relationship to his son. Rufus refuses to wear a new shoe on his crippled foot, thus revealing his rejection of the older man's easy belief that such issues as good and evil can be controlled by careful modulations of the circumstantial. When the boy is several times involved in offenses leading to police investigations, and Sheppard is forced to defend him even though he recognizes that he cannot separate truth from falsehood in these affairs, Sheppard begins to experience complexity of a kind which has so far been beyond his grasp; furthermore, it sometimes seems to him that the boy is deliberately taunting his benefactor. In a brilliantly ironic scene, it is Rufus himself who finally confronts Sheppard, who is ever more desperately determined to 'save' the boy in what has now become a contest of personal will, with the inadequacy of his own equipment for offering salvation. " 'I'm stronger than you are and I'm going to save you. The good will triumph,' " Sheppard affirms, citing the articles of the narrow canon by which he lives. But the boy returns, drawing distinctions concerning "the good" which Sheppard knows nothing about, " 'Not when it ain't true, not when it ain't right.' " Rufus's words indicate that Sheppard's world is as reductive and simplistic as that of Joy in "Good Country People," and for somewhat the same reasons. The final confrontations of the story are directed to this reduction:

"I'm not going to tell you to leave," Sheppard said. His voice was toneless, mechanical. "I'm going to save you."

Johnson thrust his head forward. "Save yourself," he hissed. "Nobody can save me but Jesus."

Sheppard laughed curtly. "You don't deceive me," he said. "I flushed that out of your head in the reformatory. I saved you from that, at least."

Near the end of the story, Sheppard is himself aware of the reversal which has occurred in relation to his former position and customary attitudes. He longs to be rid of Rufus, to be alone in the house with his son. He feels that Rufus looks at him "as if he were the guilty one, as if he were a moral leper." But one comfort remains to him: "He knew without conceit that he was a good man, that he had nothing to reproach himself with." The reversal becomes complete when Rufus, having eaten a page of the Bible and rejected Sheppard's food, leaves the house while saying to his benefactor, " 'The devil has you in his power.' "

The conclusion of the story depends upon extensions of this reversal. When Rufus is brought back to Sheppard's home by the police, he indicates that he wanted to be caught by them in order to show his contempt of the man " 'who thinks he's God.' " Then, as Rufus charges him with being a dirty atheist and having homosexual intentions, Sheppard finds himself in an altogether new position: he makes "a last desperate effort to save himself" and does so, characteristically, by his behavioristic assertion that Rufus's crippled foot, properly handled, will correct all this trouble. " 'My foot don't have a thing to do with it! ' " Rufus asserts triumphantly and then continues, in a line which parallels Ruby Turpin's unsettling vision in "Revelation," " 'The lame shall enter first! The halt'll be gathered together! ' " Sheppard, however, retains his assurance of his own goodness, even though it formulates itself in his mind with an ironic foreshadowing: he recognizes that "he had done more for Johnson than he *has* done for his own child." It consequently becomes logical, since it is an illustration of a moral principle establishing itself, that the father should discover Norton dead as a result of his attempt to reach heaven and the stars, in pursuit of the only

136 religious faith he has ever known. What occurs is in fact a recognition scene in the Aristotelian sense, depending as it does on sudden and total self-knowledge achieved, and coupled with the terrible revelation, at just the moment when the father seems about to love him, of the boy's fate:

He had stuffed his own emptiness in good works like a glutton. He had ignored his own child to feed his vision of himself. He saw the clear-eyed Devil, the sounder of hearts, leering at him from the eyes of Johnson. His image of himself shrivelled until everything was black before him. He sat there paralyzed, aghast.

He saw Norton at the telescope, all back and ears, saw his arm shoot up and wave frantically. A rush of agonizing love for the child rushed over him like a transfusion of life. The little boy's face appeared to him transformed; the image of his salvation; all light. He groaned with joy. He would make everything up to him. He would never let him suffer again. He would be mother and father. He jumped up and ran to his room, to kiss him, to tell him that he loved him, that he would never fail him again.

The light was on in Norton's room but the bed was empty. He turned and dashed up the attic stairs and at the top reeled back like a man at the edge of a pit. The tripod had fallen and the telescope lay on the edge of the floor. A few feet over it, the child hung in the jungle of shadows, just below the beam from which he had launched his flight into space.

The reversal and the irony, then, are totally within the structure of the action and constitute the operation of a moral law. Sheppard is defeated, ultimately, by the fact that no merely temporal approach to human experience is tenable. As if to prove this, the providence of God asserts itself in the unexpected but logical turns and developments of His creation.

This is the reason why landscapes in Flannery O'Connor, visualized by the reader as they suddenly register themselves upon the conscious minds of her characters, are fraught with so much weight, for they are not really temporal landscapes, and they assert their Creator, especially to those who might prefer not to acknowledge Him. In "Revelation," when Mrs. Turpin goes to search out in the hogs the meaning of the words addressed to her in the doctor's office, "the sun was getting whiter and whiter, blanching the sky overhead so that the leaves of the hickory tree were black in the face of it." A little later in the same scene, "the sun was behind the wood, very red, looking over the paling of the trees like a farmer inspecting his own hogs." The sun appears even more compellingly in "A Temple of the Holy Ghost," expressing as it does both the child and the hermaphrodite, and representing both the breadth and complexity of creation and the meaning of suffering and Christ's compassion: "The sun was a huge red ball like an elevated Host drenched in blood and when it sank out of sight, it left a line in the sky like a red clay road hanging over the trees."

In "Greenleaf," Mrs. May, who resembles Mrs. McIntyre in "The Displaced Person" and Mrs. Cope in "A Circle in the Fire" in her fierce attachment to property, sees her whole world threatened by a bull which has wandered into her pasture. Because she treats property as if it were capable of rendering her immortal, her sense of what the bull represents, and something more, is expressed in a dream in which she becomes sharply aware of the way in which the sun changes its daily meaning and, as it were, its intention:

Half the night in her sleep she heard a sound as if some large stone were grinding a hole on the outside wall of her brain. She was walking on the inside, over a succession of beautiful rolling hills, planting her stick in front of each step. She became aware after a time that the noise was the sun trying to burn through the tree line and she stopped to watch, safe in the knowledge that it couldn't, that it had to sink the way it always did outside her property. When she first stopped it was a swollen red ball, but as she stood watching it began to narrow and pale until it looked like a bullet. Then suddenly it burst through the tree line and raced down the hill toward her. She woke up with her hand over her mouth and the same noise, diminished but distinct, in

138 her ear. It was the bull munching under her window. Mr. Greenleaf had let him out.

That sun, racing down the hill like a bullet, is paradigmatic of much that is most central and expansive, and of course enduring, in Flannery O'Connor's art.

7

Nathan A. Scott, Jr.

Judgment Marked by a Cellar:
The American Negro Writer and
the Dialectic of Despair

The interests of a black man in a cellar
Mark tardy judgment on the world's closed door.
                    —Hart Crane, "Black Tambourine."

The Negro poet Countee Cullen began his poem of 1927, "Heritage," with the question "What is Africa to me?" And as he contemplated his own removal by three centuries "From the scenes his fathers loved,/Spicy grove, cinnamon tree," the question took on for him what was manifestly an import baffling and obscure—

> Africa? A book one thumbs
> Listlessly, till slumber comes.
> Unremembered are her bats
> Circling through the night, her cats
> Crouching in the river reeds. . . .
>   . . . The tree . . .
> Budding yearly must forget
> How its past arose or set. . . .

> One three centuries removed
> From the scenes his fathers loved,
> Spicy grove, cinnamon tree,
> What is Africa to me?[1]

"What is Africa to me?" The poet's question is clearly intended to be rhetorical. And it is precisely by such a skepticism as it implies about the American Negro's dependence on the African past that the interpreter of his cultural achievements would be wise to be informed. For the gulf that the anguished "Middle Passage" of long ago established between the American Negro and his African heritage could still perhaps be inchoately felt by earlier generations, as their mothers sang "Sometimes I Feel Like a Motherless Child." But today it is a gulf too depthless even to be obscurely felt. And the ancient memories that lie at the basis of Negro experience are memories not of "bats/Circling through the night" or of "cats/Crouching in the river reeds," but are rather memories of the auction block in South Carolina or Georgia, of "strange fruit hanging from the poplar trees . . . of the gallant South," and of those costly involvements of "many thousands gone" in the bone and flesh of the American Adam. Nowhere else in the life of the human community have black men and white men touched one another so deeply and indelibly as in the bitter and nascently triumphant drama of the American experiment. And it now begins to be apparent that, despite superficial differences of color and ethnic style, a common cultural identity has been forged out of this drama that belongs equally to black and white alike, for each—in blood and in experience —is a part of the other; neither is "an Iland, intire of it selfe"; each is "a peece of the Continent" which both, together, have built; if either "bee washed away by the Sea," the other "is the less"; and neither can ever "send to know for whom the bell tolls," since it is in their steadfast abiding by each other that they have their "onely securitie."

So Negro literature, like all other modes of Negro expression—jazz and the spirituals and sorrow songs, painting and sculpture and dance, pulpit and secular oratory—is inseparably a part of American culture. Phyllis Wheatley, the Negro poet of the Revolutionary period, belongs as much to the time of Philip Freneau as the novelist Jean Toomer belongs to the time of Sherwood Anderson or as Ralph Ellison belongs to the period of Faulkner and Warren. And thus to take some measure of what is religiously decisive for the literary imagination among interpreters of Negro experience in this country is not to deal with forms of sensibility that are in any way tangential with respect to the central traditions of American literature. The Negro writer, to be sure, has been given a special subject by what has been special in the circumstances of his life in the United States. But the spiritual resources on which he has drawn for the shaping of his experience are in no essential way incommensurate with the environing Protestant culture that has provided the American imagination with its most basic materials; so the theological dimension of things that we confront in Negro literature is, in its fundamental terms, the same that we meet elsewhere in our literature, just as devious and duplicitous and just as riddled with ambiguity.

Indeed, it is precisely the tidiness of the late Randall Stewart's version of the religious issue in American literature that does so emphatically call it into question. What one is perhaps first struck by in his little book of 1958, *American Literature and Christian Doctrine*, is the consistency of his inclination toward a polemical treatment of his subject, and it may be that this is a polemicism made inevitable by the excessive fastidiousness of his theological orthodoxy. So strict in fact is this orthodoxy that one wonders if it may not be by way of being something less than orthodox. For Randall Stewart makes us feel that he had remembered T. E. Hulme's dictum about Original Sin being "the closest expression of . . . the religious attitude"—the notion that man is "a wretched creature" who "can only accomplish anything of

142 value by discipline"—and Hulme's definition of "romanticism"
as the view that "man . . . is an infinite reservoir of possibilities."[2] And, working with these counters, he puts forward
a very rigorous (and, I suspect, a far too simple) definition of
Christianity: it seemed for him to be very largely summed up
in the Pauline text, "All have sinned, and come short of the
glory of God." The Pauline stringency is, of course, very much
a part of the Christian vision; but when adherence to it is
made the single criterion of that vision, the result is a kind of
rigorism that, on the one hand, cannot envisage even the possibility, say, of Emerson by any "dint of sophistry . . . [being]
brought within the Christian fold"[3] and that, on the other
hand, is prepared to regard as essentially Christian the kind of
theatricalization of Evil into an independent world-principle
that, in much of Robert Penn Warren's work, really amounts
to something like a shrill and bitter Manicheism.

Professor Stewart's was, in other words, a very *literary* kind
of theology. And, though the modishness which the notion of
Original Sin has enjoyed in literary circles in recent years may
put us in mind of a crucial aspect of the Christian testimony,
this is not an idea that, taken by itself, furnishes a sufficient
summation of the full Christian wisdom about human existence. Indeed, when it is made, in effect, the single criterion of
the authentically Christian vision, the result, as in Randall
Stewart's book, is a drastic oversimplification of the actual
complexity of the relation of Christianity to modern culture.
Emerson, for example, is certainly a crucial case in the American tradition; and it is true, of course, as Edward Taylor said,
that, though he was "one of the sweetest creatures God ever
made," there was "a screw loose somewhere in the machinery." Yet when Mr. Stewart, in effect, sides with Edward
Taylor in the view that Emerson knew "no more of the religion
of the New Testament than Balaam's ass did of the principles
of the Hebrew grammar," he oversimplifies. For, despite all
the nonsense about the "infinitude of the private man," in

his stress upon the autonomy of the individual and in his protest against all external powers that thwart the individual soul, Emerson was making a kind of witness, however attenuated, to an authentically Christian conception of responsible selfhood. Or, again, in our own time, though Professor Stewart was certainly right in regarding the vision of evil in Faulkner and Warren as partaking of an authentically Christian vision (at least when these writers are considered in relation to the naturalistic positivism so pervasive in our period), he failed to take adequately into account the fact that theirs is, though, a vision of evil that is often so unremitting as to make them very much closer to the pure pessimism of Greek tragedy than to the full wisdom of the Christian faith, whose understanding of the depth of the human predicament has always been influenced by a penitential and redemptive motif. We might say that Faulkner and Warren often seem to *believe* in Original Sin—which is never quite the stance of the integrally Christian imagination. And just as Christianly equivocal, surely, are those "Counter-Romantics" of the nineteenth century—particularly Melville —whom Stewart wanted so sharply to oppose to the heterodoxy of Emerson and Whitman.

Randall Stewart saw, to be sure, what R. W. B. Lewis was so cogently arguing in the Fifties, that ours is a culture that may be conceived by way of the image of a debate or of an unfolding dialogue; and he also understood that one of the voices perennially opposed to the tradition of our tragic realism has been that of what Lewis calls "the party of Hope."[4] But, however inhospitably disposed one may be (for reasons of temperament or of principle) to the moral and artistic sensibility of Emerson and Thoreau and Whitman and their followers, one simply cannot go through the American tradition checking off those who belong to "the party of Hope" as heterodox and checking off the tragic realists (the Hawthornes and Melvilles and Faulkners and Warrens) as orthodox. It

144   can, of course, be done, but the procedure is not likely to make for any really useful discriminations about the actual complexities that have been operative religiously in our literature.

"The hopeful attitudes," says R. W. B. Lewis, "are phenomena . . . about which we are today somewhat embarrassed: the culture's youthful indiscretions and extravagances. We have had to get beyond such simple-minded adolescent confidence, we suppose . . . and we sometimes congratulate ourselves austerely for having settled, like adults or Europeans, upon a course of prolonged but tolerable hopelessness. We call that state of hopelessness the human condition: something we study to realize in our literature and reflect in our behavior."[5] But, as Mr. Lewis wisely reminds us, irony remains "fertile and alive" and avoids becoming merely mordant only as long as it seeks to "feed and fatten" itself on the opposite possibilities of hope. "The new hopelessness is, paradoxically," he says, "as simple-minded as innocence," and its "chilling skepticism . . . represents one of the modes of death."[6] Nor is this cautionary word applicable only to our contemporary situation: it also has, I believe, a certain relevance to our entire tradition. Mr. Lewis is surely right in arguing, as he does in *The American Adam*, that our whole literature, from Cooper to Faulkner, may be viewed under the aspect of the myth of Adam—a second Adam, who, in a new Paradise, must be painfully initiated into the difficult complexities of the moral life. He demonstrates, with great subtlety of insight, how persistently this myth has provided American literature with its constitutive themes, and he indicates how frequently the portrait that emerges is of innocence and naiveté unequipped to resist the crises and distempers of life. Indeed, it is in the discoveries born out of this disconcertion that our tragic realism has had its main source. But the trouble has been that the American Adam has sometimes been so deeply unhinged by the discovery of evil that he has, in his shock, been led to elevate evil into a principle coeval with God

himself. And thus it is that that "blackness" which Melville
found in Hawthorne becomes, in Melville's phrase, "ten times
black" and becomes the blackness of Manicheism, a blackness,
as Mr. Lewis says, that represents one of the modes of death.

In his brilliant book *The American Novel and Its Tradition*,
the late Richard Chase is at one point remarking the "great
practical sanity" of the English novel, the fact that it has
rarely included "oddity, distortion of personality, dislocations
of normal life, recklessness of behavior, malignancy of motive."[7] And this puts him in mind of the difficulty that F. R.
Leavis has, in *The Great Tradition*, in fitting the author of
Wuthering Heights into the great central line of English fiction,
the line of Jane Austen, of George Eliot, of Conrad and James
and Lawrence. He quotes the passage in which Dr. Leavis admits that this "astonishing work seems to me a kind of sport"
and then says:

Of course Mr. Leavis is right; in relation to the great tradition
of the English novel, *Wuthering Heights* is indeed a sport. But
suppose it were discovered that *Wuthering Heights* was written
by an American of New England Calvinist or Southern Presbyterian
background. The novel would be astonishing and unique no
matter who wrote it or where. But if it were an American novel
it would not be a sport; it has too close an affinity with too many
American novels, and among them some of the best. Like many
of the [major] fictions . . . [in the American tradition]
Wuthering Heights proceeds from an imagination that is
essentially melodramatic, that operates among radical
contradictions and renders reality indirectly or poetically. . . .[8]

And, of course, Richard Chase's instinct about Emily Brontë
and her assimilability into American tradition is absolutely
right, for her kind of dark, narrow, sensationalistic profundity
is most assuredly not at all a strange thing in our own literature; the story of Heathcliffe and Catherine Linton has far
more in common with *The Marble Faun*, *The Scarlet Letter*,
Pierre, *Pudd'nhead Wilson*, *Sanctuary*, and *The Sun Also*

146 *Rises* than it has with any of the representative texts in English fiction. "*Wuthering Heights*," says E. M. Forster in his little book *Aspects of the Novel*, "is filled with sound—storm and rushing wind."⁹ And, at a distance, this might also be one's impression of much of American literature—eerie and frightening, mysterious and ghost-ridden, exposed to all the atmospheric tumults of the storm and the rushing wind.

So it is no wonder that not only the English Gothicism of Emily Brontë but also the German Gothicism of Franz Kafka seem to be close to us and to be a part of us: indeed, as Leslie Fiedler reminds us, Kafka's major posthumous successes have "belonged almost more to the history of our literature than his own."¹⁰ "The terror of which I write," said Edgar Poe, "is not of Germany, but of the soul." And it is into this perilous interior that we are taken in Melville's *Pierre*, in Stephen Crane's *The Red Badge of Courage*, in Djuna Barnes' *Nightwood*, in John Hawkes's *The Cannibal*, and in James Purdy's *Malcolm*. In book after book after book, in fact, in the American tradition the glow of the scene is lurid and nocturnal: the protagonists are exhibited (in Faulkner's words [*Light in August*]) as engendering "so much more than [they] can or should have to bear"; the human adventure appears to be "an ironic and tragic affair that is beyond human rule and misrule";¹¹ and the authorial intelligence that lies behind these books seems to be one which "believes in original sin, but not in divine love."¹²

Now, in the case of Hawthorne, Melville was inclined to suggest that "this great power of blackness . . . derives its force from its appeals to that Calvinistic sense of Innate Depravity and Original Sin, from whose visitations, in some shape or other, no deeply thinking mind is always and wholly free."¹³ And it may well be that it is just here, in Melville's essay on "Hawthorne and His *Mosses*," that we have the most important single insight ever to be achieved into the nature of what is theologically determinative of the main slant and bias of the American imagination. It is true, of course, that, by the time of Hawthorne and Melville, American Calvinism in the form of the Puritan movement had long since lost its original unity and power as a creative force in religious history. The process of the dissolution is sensitively traced in Richard Niebuhr's *The Kingdom of God in America*,[14] where it is shown how, following the period of the "Great Awakening," the original radicalism petered out, as a result of institutionalizing and secularizing influences. Indeed, it is not an *over*simplification of our theological history to say that, between the time of Jonathan Edwards and Reinhold Niebuhr, there is not a single theologian in the American tradition of really commanding importance, none, that is, whose achievement makes him eligible for that modern pantheon which embraces such Europeans as Schleiermacher and Kierkegaard and Ritschl and Barth. And certainly in the period of Melville and Hawthorne the Christian enterprise in this country could offer nothing more, theologically, than the equally flaccid options of Charles Grandison Finney on the one hand or Theodore Parker and Ralph Waldo Emerson on the other.

Yet, for all of the dissolution of high Calvinism that had been accomplished by the middle years of the nineteenth century, Melville's instinct about his friend was right, for the great power of blackness in Hawthorne does indeed derive "its force from its appeals to that Calvinistic sense of Innate Depravity and Original Sin," and so does it have the same derivation in Melville himself—as it does also in Faulkner or in Warren in our own day. For though it is true that the "enthusiasm" of the Finneys and Moodys and Billy Grahams on the one hand and the progressivistic optimism and positive thinking of the Emersons and Mary Baker Eddys and Norman Vincent Peales on the other have, in various ways, been the sources of the main movements of popular religion in America over the past hundred years, it is also true that classic Calvinism entered deeply into the national consciousness, and

148   it has in fact found its best expressions in our imaginative
literature. Writers like Hawthorne and Melville and Faulkner
and Warren have not, of course, seen *what* the great Puritans
saw, but they have seen things *as* their great forebears saw
them,[15] and one feels that it is this great heritage—"with its
grand metaphors of election and damnation, its opposition of
the Kingdom of Light and the Kingdom of Darkness, its
eternal and autonomous contraries of good and evil"[16]—one
feels that it is this great heritage which provides them with
their fundamental terms of reference. For theirs is an imagination of human existence as irremediably hazardous and
problematic: it is an imagination extremist and melodramatic
whose themes are improbable and negative and horrific; the
themes of the Gothic tale of terror. And the tradition that
descends from these figures is one filled with "radical malad-
justments and contradictions,"[17] a tradition "less interested in
redemption than in . . . the eternal struggle between good and
evil, less interested in incarnation and reconciliation than in
alienation and disorder."[18]

   This is the sort of secularized Calvinism that constitutes a
large part of the religious inheritance whose pressure is felt
by the literary artist in American culture, and it is an inheritance felt with an especial force by the Negro writer. He is, of
course, as alienated from the official usages of the Christian
tradition as his white counterpart in the intellectual community tends to be, perhaps even far more profoundly so. The
cliché-ridden mentality of popular journalism and sociology
supposes that nowhere in our culture does an integrally
Christian vision of things have a stronger residual life than
amongst the Negro populace, and this may still be true to a
considerable extent of the black peasantry of the rural South.
But there is much which would indicate that the Negro proletarian participates in the spiritual rootlessness of industrial
society quite as deeply as does the modern worker generally.
And the Negro intellectual has long since ceased, in any signif-

icant degree, to approximate the astonishing picture that Professor Edward Shils offers of the religious situation of the Indian intellectual. In the brilliant account presented a few years ago in *The Sewanee Review* of "The Culture of the Indian Intellectual,"[19] Mr. Shils tells us that in contemporary India, amongst intellectuals, religious agnosticism is an inconsequential minority position and that the historic religious traditions continue robustly to live on there in today's intellectual community. And he maintains this to be so, even though insisting at the same time on the profound impact of Westernizing influence. It is a surprising line of argument which is not altogether convincing. But should it turn out that, in this regard, Mr. Shils is more right than wrong, the religious situation of the Indian intellectual would then have to be acknowledged as differing most radically from that of the American Negro intellectual whose painful experience of the hiatus in a Christian culture between ethical profession and practice has taught him to understand religion in the terms of "ideology" and, if pressed on the point, to say in effect, as James Baldwin does, that "God . . . is white"[20] and that "whoever wishes to become a truly moral human being . . . must first divorce himself from all the prohibitions, crimes and hypocrisies of the Christian church."[21]

This is not, of course, to say that the Negro writer has not found in the mythopoeic idioms and iconology of the folk religion of Negro Protestantism a rich vein of dramatic material: for the poetry of James Weldon Johnson and Langston Hughes, and the fiction of Cullen and Zora Neale Hurston and James Baldwin—to mention only a few instances—clearly have this kind of dependence. But, even in so beautifully executed and moving a book as Weldon Johnson's *God's Trombones* (1927), with its brilliant employment of the rhetoric of the old Negro pulpit, one feels the writer's position *vis-à-vis* his *mythos* to be that of a kind of archaeologist: the very shrewdness of the mimicry with which an archaic rhetoric is

150 rendered, the almost too brilliant expertise of it, carries a suggestion of the distance at which the poet stands from the implied protagonist of the verse. And one feels much the same distance between artist and *mythos* in such a later book as James Baldwin's *Go Tell It On the Mountain* (1953), whose evocation of the world of the Harlem store-front church is, in the terms of prose fiction, as nimble a performance as Weldon Johnson's of a quarter-century earlier in the dramatic lyric. Though both writers—along with many others who might also be cited—use a religious tradition, they make us feel that what they themselves are most truly in contact with is a detritus of sentiment and rhetoric which is the last residuum of pieties effective now only in the degree to which they provide a sophisticated artist with a sort of framework for his "romance." Their distance, in short, from the position of a genuinely Christian writer (who is something else again— as in the case of a Claudel, a Mauriac, an Auden—from the writer who simply raids a religious tradition for dramatic machinery) is perhaps something like the distance between the Thornton Wilder of *Heaven's My Destination* and *Our Town* and the Eliot of *Ash Wednesday* and the *Quartets*.

So the Negro writer, for all of his occasional captivation by the charm of folk religion, represents no great exception to the general secularity of his intellectual class. Indeed, it may well be the profundity of his alienation from the Christian tradition that has left him so susceptible to the deracinative effects of the experience of exclusion which is our culture's decisive bequest to its Negro members. Yet, in a way, it is precisely this experience that prepares him to order his world in accordance with the myth of the "wounded Adam" which is a fundamental archetype figuring in that secularized Calvinism which our writers enter into the more deeply as they absorb the air and atmosphere of our literature.

In Brockden Brown's *Arthur Mervyn*, in Hawthorne's *The Scarlet Letter*, in Melville's *Billy Budd*, in James's *The Prin-*

cess Casamassima, in Dreiser's *An American Tragedy*, in Bellow's *Augie March*, in James Purdy's *Malcolm*—as in Richard Wright's *Native Son* and Ralph Ellison's *Invisible Man* and James Baldwin's *Another Country*—this is an Adam (the "wounded Adam") who is (normally) a provincial and who, with "great expectations," seeks to enter a world which, even if it is no vaster in size than Hester Prynne's village or Billy Budd's ship, is a complex and deviously ordered place. This is an Adam who comes from without the precincts of human intermingling and is "morally prior"[22] to all that, being unencumbered by familial or social attachments—and he is a stranger in the world, he is an "outsider," because he is unstained by the world's improbity. He approaches the world not with any sort of fastidious distaste but with an enormous yearning and aspiration, for he sees it initially as a proving ground where all things may be added unto him: it is "the good earth" and a world of promises, and he applies his full energy toward winning what will be for him the great prize—namely, some definitive authentication of his really belonging to the human polity that he confronts. He wants an acknowledged "place," he wants to be accommodated. So he advances hopefully into a complex order of things the inner logic of which he does not fully grasp. But though he may succeed in doing nothing more than "leaving his mark upon the world . . . [as] a sign in which conquest may later become possible for the survivors,"[23] his own last state is likely to be greatly different from the first. For sometimes, like Antaeus, the wounded Adam—whom the American imagination likes so much to contemplate—does not win access to a deeper strength through his encounter with the world, the moral weather of Experience being a climate of gale in which Innocence is bound to be undone. And even if his "initiation" is *into* society rather than *away* from it,[24] the process is likely to exact an enormous cost, so that something is lost of that first fine flush of buoyancy and good cheer with which the hero began his voyage, the maturity that he achieves being a thing of stoical sobriety and resignation, an affair of deflation and disenchantment; the wisdom of experience, in other words, proves purchasable only by the loss of something bright and lovely which is a natural *donnée* of that "simple genuine self" which Emerson regarded as "the plain old Adam . . . against the whole world."

Now it is this myth of the American as Adam, hectored and wounded by "the world," that Leslie Fiedler and Richard Lewis and numerous other recent students of American tradition have taught us to discern as having played an executive role in the shaping of our literature. And what I want now to suggest is that one of the significant bodies of evidence to be adduced in this connection is that which is comprised by the work of Negro writers, of whom the chief exemplars today are doubtless the late Richard Wright and Ralph Ellison and James Baldwin. Knowing so intimately as they do the world of the insulted and the rejected, theirs is an experience of life in the United States that has bred in them a habit of reflection whose natural fulcrum is the dialectic of innocence and experience: the "wounded Adam" is bone of their bone and flesh of their flesh. And indeed it is precisely in the extreme situation to which American history has committed these writers that we may see with an especial clarity a particular turn which the literary imagination in this country has been recurrently tempted to take in its broodings on Adam's unlucky fate. It is the turn which, as Richard Lewis reminds us, is classically adumbrated in Melville's incident of "The Try-Works" in *Moby-Dick*.

It will be recalled that on a certain evening, towards midnight, Ishmael is taking his turn at the *Pequod's* helm. And, from the stern, he looks down on the crew below, between the foremast and mainmast, where they are gathered around two vast boiling cauldrons into which they are pitching great masses of blubber, as "the wind howled on, and the sea leaped, and the ship groaned and dived, and yet steadfastly shot in her red hell further into the blackness. . . ." As Ishmael gazes down into this gloomy pit, "now and then made ghastly by flashes of redness," he falls off to sleep, just for a moment: then, just as quickly, he wakens, and, before he is even aware that he has been dozing, he becomes in a moment's flash "horribly conscious of something fatally wrong." Then it is he realizes that, in his sleep, he has swung the tiller around, so that, now, he is able to swing it about only just in time to keep the vessel from flying up into the wind and possibly capsizing. "How glad and how grateful the relief from this unnatural hallucination of the night," sighs Ishmael the narrator, in retrospect. Then Melville points the moral:

Look not too long in the face of the fire, O man! . . .Turn not thy back to the compass . . . believe not the artificial fire, when its redness makes all things look ghastly. To-morrow, in the natural sun, the skies will be bright; those who glared like devils in the forking flames, the morn will show in far other, at least gentler, relief; the glorious, golden, glad sun, the only true lamp—all others but liars!

But now it is precisely this dangerous course, of looking too long into the face of fire, that the "wounded Adam" has often been tempted to take: indeed, the sign of his wound is just this fascination with the demonic, this "hypnosis by evil."[25] And, amongst the many rich examples that American literature affords, none is more deserving of attention than that body of testimony which has come from our ablest Negro writers who are, all of them, most deeply stirred by the myth of the American Adam, more especially by the myth of the "wounded Adam"—and, in the very best of them, what is perhaps of the highest interest is the degree to which "the relief from this unnatural hallucination of the night" is just barely managed, through a feat of imaginative transcendence. They all have a deep knowledge of what Mr. Auden was telling us at the end of the 'thirties, in the famous sentence of his

154 poem "September 1, 1939," that "We must love one another or die"—and it is the general failure of love that prompts their rage, their sense of being "lost in a haunted wood."

It is surely in the inflamed and socially discarnate wraiths at the center of Richard Wright's fiction that we encounter the most drastic instances of the wounded Adam in American literature. In "Long Black Song," one of the stories in his collection of 1938, *Uncle Tom's Children*, the husband of a Negro woman who has been seduced by a white salesman says: "The white folks ain never gimme a chance! They ain never give no black man a chance! There ain nothing in yo whole life yuh kin keep from em!. . . . Ahm gonna be hard like they is! So hep me Gawd, Ahm gonna be *hard!* When they come fer me Ahm gonna *be* here!" And this is precisely the posture of the young Chicago Negro whose story is told in *Native Son* (1940), the novel that made Wright the first Negro writer to win a major reputation in American literary life. Bigger Thomas is one who intends to "be hard": indeed, as he says, "Every time I think about it I feel like somebody's poking a red-hot iron down my throat." So it is with a sullen suspiciousness that he faces the Chicago philanthropist who takes him off the relief rolls by hiring him as a chauffeur. And it is with an even greater skepticism that he views his employer's daughter and her Communist sweetheart who make gestures of fraternity toward him by inviting him to join them in a café as an equal. But this is a relation that never becomes genuinely complicated, for, at the end of their first evening together, the girl is so intoxicated that Bigger, having been entrusted with seeing her home, has to carry her bodily from the family automobile to her bedroom—into which her blind mother comes suddenly, just in the moment when he is contemplating a sexual act. In order to prevent the mother's knowing that he and Mary are in the room, he smothers the girl; then, in his panic, he stuffs her body into the furnace—which, in turn, leads eventually to his second crime, now against his

mistress Bessie, to whom he confesses the first deed and whom
he must finally remove to prevent her betraying him to the
police. But he cannot ultimâtely avoid his nemesis and is at
last captured on a South Side tenement rooftop as a raging
mob clamors for his life in the street below.

Now the engine Wright desperately relied upon to whip
this lurid fairy-tale into some semblance of probability was
the courtroom defense of Bigger by his Jewish lawyer, Mr.
Max—who tells us that, though there are no corpses, Bigger
has committed countless murders long before the assault on
Mary Dalton:

"This Negro boy's entire attitude toward life is a *crime*! The hate
and fear which we have inspired in him, woven by our civilization
into the very structure of his consciousness, into his blood and
bones, into the hourly functioning of his personality, have
become the justification of his existence.

"Every time he comes in contact with us, he kills! . . . Every
thought he thinks is potential murder. . . . Every hope is a plan
for insurrection. Every glance of the eye is a threat. *His very
existence is a crime against the state!*"

And, what is more, we are told that we have only to "multiply
Bigger Thomas twelve million times, allowing for environ-
mental and temperamental variations, and for those Negroes
who are completely under the influence of the Church, and
you have the psychology of the Negro people."

Thus it is that, in offering a depraved and inhuman beast
as the comprehensive image of the American Negro, the novel
shows itself to be overwhelmed finally by the very cancer it
wants to cauterize. For, from the moment, on its first page,
when Bigger is awakened by the *Brrrrriiiiiiinnnnnnnng*! of his
alarm clock, until his "faint, wry, bitter smile" of farewell at
Mr. Max on the final page, the novel is controlled by precisely
those hopeless assumptions about Negro life which elicited
its rage, and its protagonist's sense of his own identity is
formed by just that image of himself which, as it lives in the

larger culture, has caused his despair. So long, in other words, had Richard Wright looked into the face of fire that, when he turned away, to give dramatic substance to the hue and cry he wanted to sound, it was his tendency himself to brutalize the creatures of his imagination. Enraged as he was by the indignities that had been heaped on the Negro's head in this country, he wanted, as it were, to hold "a loaded pistol at the head of the white world while . . . [muttering] between clenched teeth: 'Either you grant us equal rights as human beings or else this is what will happen.' "[26] So, as in the wronged husband of "Long Black Song," he had to make his characters "hard"; and in thus sweeping them into the raging abysses of violent criminality, he forged an image of *la présence noire* that is in no great way removed from the wild and lickerish nigger who inhabits the demented imagination of the racial paranoiac.

Nor was this a pathos that Wright was ever able to escape. Even in the Fifties, after his long years of residence in Paris and tutelage under French existentialism, he was still presenting the American Negro as a wounded innocent who is an outsider, not only in a sociological sense but also, and more decisively, in a moral sense as well. *The Outsider* (1953), which is the most important book of this late period of his career, has as its protagonist Cross Damon, a half-educated young intellectual who bears the Negro's ancestral burden of rejection and marginality; but his concern with what is socially problematic in his situation is but one phase of a deeper concern with what is metaphysically problematic in human life. He is a man whose sense of the world has been formed by that tradition of philosophic radicalism that runs from Nietzsche to contemporary existentialists like Heidegger and Sartre, and he is thus particularly alert to the religious vacuum which this tradition has asserted to be at the heart of modern experience. He no longer sleeps in the old myths of the Greeks and the Jews: he has arrived at that chilling conclusion of modern nihilism, that nothing is to be preferred to anything else; and for him, this means that the dreadful burden which man must bear today is the burden of freedom, the burden, as he says, of being "nothing in particular," except what he chooses through his actions to become. This is why panic sometimes drapes the world which he looks out upon, for what he knows himself to confront is "the empty possibility of action," and he also knows that he can do what he damn well pleases on this earth. For God is dead, and everything is therefore permitted. It is this "dreadful objectivity" to which he is given access by the alienation from our culture which he suffers as a Negro.

So that night when Cross walks into the room where the Fascist nigger-hater Herndon and the Communist Blount are fighting and bludgeons them both to death, he is "not taking sides . . . not preferring the lesser evil." For, in the world that he knows, there are no sides to be taken; and his act is simply "a sweeping and supreme gesture of disdain and disgust with both of them!" Like Camus' Caligula, his mission as an outsider is to reveal to mankind that the human City is really a jungle and that all the disciplines and restraints of civilization are "just screens which men have used" to throw a kind of "veneer of order" over the disorder that still seethes beneath the surface. But since, as it appears, this is a mission that cannot be accomplished apart from terrorism, Wright's conclusion of 1953 entailed essentially the same mischievousness that had been implicit thirteen years earlier in *Native Son*, the notion that the natural life-movement of the Negro who bears the full burden of his situation is toward a great blasting moment of supreme destruction. Bigger Thomas is an inarticulate proletarian who enacts his role unthinkingly, whereas Cross Damon, having read his Nietzschean primers, accepts his mission with deliberateness and in the spirit of a kind of inverted messianism—but this is the only significant difference between them, for both aim, as it were, at getting outside of history altogether, through an act of consummate violence. Like Conrad's Kurtz, Cross does, to be sure, behold at last "the horror," as he gaspingly admits to Houston, the prosecuting attorney, a moment before his death; but he has, nevertheless, tasted the terrible joy of his murderous orgasm: he has burst the belt and been "hard" and won through at last to the unhistorical realm of the dream—which is of revenge.

So, in the case of Richard Wright, the myth of the wounded Adam leads to a *mystique* of gratuitous violence—which there was never any large chance of his transcending, given his immoderate and melodramatic imagination of the world as "split in two, a white world and a black one, the white one being separated from the black by a million psychological miles." What begins, though, to be a little distressing is that his brilliant younger contemporary James Baldwin should have seen so clearly how unpromising was the impasse at which Wright finally arrived—as was evinced in his *Partisan Review* essay on Wright of 1949 ("Everybody's Protest Novel")—and yet should now himself, apparently, be heading towards something like the same detour.

Mr. Baldwin's essay on "Everybody's Protest Novel" at the end of the Forties marked his entrance into American literary life, and, in what was virtually his first major declaration, he was eager to describe and to reject that fear of the rich, complex particularity of the human individual which he had found to be a defining characteristic of "protest" fiction, from Harriet Stowe's *Uncle Tom's Cabin* to Laura Hobson's *Gentleman's Agreement*; it is, he insisted, a literature that moves wholly within the bloodless abstractions of ethical rhetoric; it asserts by implication that "it is [the human being's] categorization alone which is real and which cannot be transcended." And, for all of the simplicity of its good intentions, it is a literature which is mischief-making, in so far as the very hotness of its temperature may persuade its victims to accept the dehumanization which it would practice upon them: indeed, said

Mr. Baldwin, Bigger Thomas, in admitting "the possibility
of his being sub-human," is "Uncle Tom's descendant, flesh
of his flesh. . . ."

Mr. Baldwin's initial purpose, then, as he said in this
essay, was to insist that the task of the novelist is "revelation"
of "the disquieting complexity of ourselves." And one suspects
that, basically, his disaffection from Richard Wright was
caused not so much by the element of "protest" in Wright's
fiction—for that has perennially been an element of the greatest literature, from the *Antigone* to *The Possessed,* from *Don
Quixote* to *Doctor Faustus*—as by Wright's incorrigible commitment to a violent and narrow naturalism, to an aesthetic
which (in its descent from Norris and Dreiser to Dos Passos
and Farrell) required the artist to view the human individual
as simply an epiphenomenon of social and political process, of
the pressures and counter-pressures of History. Indeed, it
may well be that the acute discomfort with the aesthetics of
naturalistic fiction that the young Baldwin could feel, and that
Wright could not, was in some measure a result of the greater
internalization in the younger man of a Christian background.
The religion on which Mr. Baldwin was nurtured as a young-
ster in Harlem was, of course, as he reports on it in various
essays, a narrow and fanatical thing, breeding intensely destructive emotions and a most unwholesome asceticism: it was
the very tag end of Protestant sectarian pietism, made absurdly
stern and exacting in its ethic by what was neurasthenic in the
experience of the black proletarian. Yet, for all of its bilious-
ness and obscurantism, this was a religion bound to inculcate
in one receiving his early formation under its auspices a sense
of the multi-leveled mystery of the individual human life,
and a sense of the impossibility of containing this mystery
within the reductionist formulae of a Dreiser or a Dos Passos—
or a Wright.

So, in his first book, *Go Tell It on the Mountain*—which
proved to be one of the finest American novels of the 1950's

160   —Mr. Baldwin, instead of hurling forth some hard-boiled and
torrential blast of strident "sociology," chose as his form what
German criticism has designated as the *Bildungsroman*: he
undertook to produce a novel of development, and thus his
theme—autobiographical undoubtedly—is the formation of a
boy's character, a sensitive Negro boy who has to find his way
toward some liberating sense of his own human possibilities,
in the repressive atmosphere of a primitive religion of Jesus
and Satan fanatically celebrated in the Harlem storefront
church (the Temple of the Fire Baptized) and fiercely admin-
istered in the family. The young hero of the novel, John
Grimes, as he faces the oppressively confining world of his
family and its fanatical religion and the terrible backwater of
Harlem, decides that he must revolt: "He would not be like
his father, or his father's father. He would have another life."
He is standing one day in Central Park before a slope which

stretched upward, and above it the brilliant sky, and beyond
it, cloudy, and far away, he saw the skyline of New York. He did
not know why, but there arose in him an exultation and a sense
of power, and he ran up the hill like an engine, or a madman,
willing to throw himself headlong into the city that glowed before
him. . . . For it was his; the inhabitants of the city had told him
it was his; he had but to run down, crying, and they would
take him to their hearts and show him wonders his eyes had
never seen.

But this dream never comes to fulfillment, or at least not to
a fulfillment so simple as that which the boy first imagines.
For John is finally swept by his great need for reconciliation
with his family and with his ancestral community, by his guilt
over his awakening sexuality, by the unsubduable propensity
for religious hysteria implanted in him by his nurture—he is
finally hurled by all these forces onto the Threshing-Floor and
swept into a high fever of spiritual convulsion in The Temple
of the Fire Baptized. And though in his moment of seizure an
"ironic voice insisted . . . that he rise from that filthy floor if he

did not want to become like all the other niggers," and though he feels himself, as it were, in a grave, he beholds in this grave "the despised and rejected, the wretched and the spat upon, the earth's offscouring." In this moment the trouble-laden history of his father and mother, of Aunt Florence, of Praying Mother Washington and Sister McCandless and Sister Price, becomes as never before a living reality for him: "their dread testimony" and "their desolation" become his, and he knows that, only as he passes through their darkness, will he find his right course. So, at the novel's close, after the fearful night of his conversion experience is over, he walks at dawn through the filthy streets of Harlem, "among the saints, he, John . . . one of their company now." His soul is filled with gladness, for he has sworn to fight the good fight. And what is implied is that the vista he beheld that day from his "mountain" in Central Park will finally be achieved only by way of a pilgrimage involving an ascent of that Mount of Primal Pain immemorially trodden by Hagar's children.

The book—which is one of the most tightly constructed and beautifully written novels of our period—is not, to be sure, a "protest novel," but it does become for Mr. Baldwin, finally, a passionate gesture of identification with his people. And it can now be seen in retrospect as marking the path he was increasingly to follow in the years to come. It was succeeded, of course, by the essay in the morally fancy punctilio of Paris homosexualism which we were given in the novel of 1956, *Giovanni's Room*; and, despite Mr. Baldwin's deep engagement with the homosexual life, this is a book that strikes us as a deflection, as a kind of detour. But, throughout the Fifties, he was busily engaged in journalism, writing about books and the theatre and his travels and various aspects of the American scene. And in all these various pieces—collected in *Notes of a Native Son* (1955) and *Nobody Knows My Name* (1961)—as he probed more deeply the meaning of Negro experience in this country, his own chosen role came more and more to be

162   that of racial ideologue and of Chief Barrister for the black multitudes at the bar of the American conscience. Whereas the pronoun of the first person in his earliest writings had expressed a passionately sensuous and individual intelligence, it comes increasingly in these years to take on a vast and vaguely menacing collectivist aura, so that the "I" we encounter on his pages begins no longer to stand for the intensely interesting man, James Baldwin, but for all Negroes everywhere, both the living and the dead. By some twist of his own nature and under the pressure of the rising Negro insurgency, he began himself to be "the Negro *in extremis*, a [veritable] virtuoso of ethnic suffering, defiance and aspiration."[27] This mounting militancy reaches its highest pitch in the essay of 1963, *The Fire Next Time*, and in the novel *Another Country* (1962) and the play *Blues for Mr. Charlie* (1964), which want to score many of the points already established in the polemical tracts. Here, the loss of poise that threatens is uncountered by any such nonchalance and stability of perspective as might be afforded by a firm structure of religious belief. Mr. Baldwin's writing is, of course, both in his essays and in his fiction, abundantly embellished with religious paraphernalia —and a large part of the remarkable beauty of *Go Tell It on the Mountain* derives from its brilliant employment of Biblical idiom and imagery. But one could hardly argue that in this book the stuff of experience is being conceived Christianly, as in Graham Greene's *The Power and the Glory* or Bernanos' *The Diary of a Country Priest* or John Updike's *The Centaur*: the novel, in its conception of character and in its structure of incident, strikes us rather, at the level of systematic ideas, as being far more dependent on Freud and William James than on Pascal or Luther or Kierkegaard or Niebuhr. I did, to be sure, speak earlier of the greater internalization of Christian background in Mr. Baldwin than in Richard Wright, for, in the latter's case, what we face, in the spiritual landscape of his fiction, is a world utterly desacralized, a world in which the

traditions of Christian belief and experience are as if they had never been, so uninvolved are they in the pressing existential reality of human endeavor. At least, in the case of Mr. Baldwin, it needs to be said that the memory of Christianity is still discernibly a factor in his imaginative universe, bequeathing him, if nothing more, such a sense, as Richard Wright seems never to have had, of the radical mystery incarnate in the human creature. But when Mr. Baldwin says, as he did a few years ago in an address at Kalamazoo College ("In Search of a Majority" in *Nobody Knows My Name*), that "to be with God is really to be involved with some enormous, overwhelming desire, and joy" and that he conceives "of God, in fact, as a means of liberation and not a means to control others"—when he speaks in this way, he makes us feel that he is undoubtedly a man of genuine religious sensibility, but (as is indicated by the lumpily "homemade" quality of the language) a sensibility that is quite out of touch with any of the great traditions of Christian theology and spirituality (despite his familiarity with the Bible and his very great knowledgeableness about a particular mode of pietistic folk religion). So, in the last analysis, he has no resource for distancing himself in any way religiously from the kind of secularized Calvinism which, as a writer, is his American inheritance; and, as his work of recent years has begun to indicate, he is, finally, very nearly helpless before the power of that myth which is so much a part of this inheritance—namely, the myth of the wounded Adam. Indeed, it is just this that would seem to be so much in evidence in the tendency of his essays of the last decade—in making the pronoun "I" at once personal and collective and in thus merging a personal plight with the larger racial plight of the American Negro—to make their author (his own loneliness, his own alienation) the real beneficiary of the pity which is ostensibly sought for an entire people. "Alas, Poor Richard," says Mr. Baldwin in the title of his most recent essay on Richard Wright —and in that phrase, one feels, he distances himself too much

164 from his first sponsor and patron, for, at last, both are to be seen as sustained by a single myth, a single mode of sensibility and belief.

Though Ralph Ellison has published thus far only one novel—*Invisible Man* of 1953—his achievement as an artist strikes us as being far less in question than either that of Richard Wright or of Mr. Baldwin, the three of them together being the most important Negro writers yet to enter American literary life. In a time when so many of our ablest novelists have chosen to seek their effects by the unsaid and the withheld, by the muted voice and the scrupulously reserved style, Mr. Ellison, like Faulkner and Warren, is notable in part for being unafraid to howl and rage and bellow with laughter over the fate of man. And surely it is the uninhibited exhilaration and suppleness of his rhetoric that is a main source of that richness of texture which so distinguishes his book. But sheer verbal energy alone cannot produce a fiction that requires to be regarded as a work of art; there must also be the gift for conveying what Henry James insisted on, namely, "the direct impression" of life itself. And, in this, Mr. Ellison is superbly talented. Indeed, one of our richest satisfactions in reading his book comes from the sense of immersion in all the concrete materialities of Negro life: one hears the very buzz and hum of Harlem in the racy, pungent speech of his West Indians and native hipsters; one sees the fearful nonchalance of the zootsuiter and hears the terrible anger of the black nationalist on his streetcorner platform; and all the *grotesquerie* in the opening account of the dreary little backwater of a remote Southern Negro college has in it a certain kind of empirically absolute rightness. The book is packed full of the acutest observations of the manners and idioms and human styles that comprise the ethos of Negro life in the American metropolis, and it gives us such a sense of social fact as can be come by nowhere in the manuals of academic sociology; all this is done with the ease that comes from enormous expertness of craft, from deep intimacy of knowledge, and love.

Mr. Ellison suppresses his middle name—which is "Waldo" and which gives a certain tricky rightness to the fact that for him too, like so many other writers in the American tradition, the basic pattern of experience is something like Emerson's "simple genuine self against the whole world."[28] But, in his version of the Adamic myth, though the "simple genuine self" is "wounded" by the world, the result is neither a descent into the "cheap grace"[29] of self-pity (as in Mr. Baldwin) nor a nihilistic blast of destructive violence (as in Wright)—but, rather, it is a step forward into a further maturity, into a deepened awareness of the essential solitude that is a part of the human fate. And his hero is not undone by his discovery; indeed, by an act of transcendence, he comes to realize that, though his passage through the world has involved the special ordeals that are a part of being a Negro in the United States, he can nevertheless, as a result of what he has discovered about the basic human condition, in some measure speak "on the lower frequencies" for all men.

The protagonist of Mr. Ellison's novel is a young American Negro who has to pick his perilous way through the irrationalities of a culture which has made of him an "invisible man," and his whole effort is an effort to wrest an acknowledgment, to achieve visibility. He starts, in other words, from a point outside the world. We see him first as a timid boy about to be graduated from his high school in a southern town, valedictorian of his class, with an earnest little speech on the virtues of humility that is reminiscent of Booker Washington. Along with some of his schoolmates, he is invited to a smoker where the leading white citizens are to hear his speech and award him a scholarship. But the boys do not know in advance what the nature of the entertainment is to be that night; they are brought before a lush and naked blonde, and threatened by the crowd if they look and if they fail to look. Then, after being blindfolded, they are forced to stage a "battle royal" among themselves, punching and kicking one another for the obscene titillation of this degenerate mob—and then they are

166   made to scramble for coins on an electrified rug. Finally, the valedictorian delivers his speech about humility and his gratitude to his white benefactors. The boy later dreams that, on opening the briefcase that these gentlemen had presented to him along with his scholarship, he found an inscription: "To Whom It May Concern: Keep This Nigger-Boy Running." And so indeed he shall be running in the years to come, "skidding around corners and dashing down alleys, endlessly harried by the cops and the crooks of the world, endlessly hurrying in search of whatever it is that can sanctify human existence."[30]

The next stage in this *picaro's* journey is a Southern Negro college, where, inadvertently, on a certain day he exposes a visiting white trustee from the North to a Negro farmer's incestuous relation with his daughter and to the local Negro gin-mill—and, as a result, is ousted from the college by its unctuous and cynical president, as a punishment for his having allowed the college's donor to see what white folks are not supposed to see.

Then, the young man moves on to New York, where, after becoming involved—again, inadvertently—as a scab in labor violence, he is taken up by the communistic "Brotherhood" after delivering an impassioned speech in the streets before a crowd watching the eviction of an aged Negro couple from their Harlem tenement flat; his job with the "Brotherhood" is to *organize* the sullenness of Harlem Negroes. But he soon discovers that the Negro's cause is only being used to promote "the line." So, at last, in disillusionment, after a furious race riot in the Harlem streets, he dives through a manhole, down into a cellar, for a period of "hibernation." He has tried the way of "humility," of being a "good Negro"; he has tried to find room for himself in American industry, to become a good cog in the complex of the technological machine; he has attempted to attach himself to leftist politics—he has tried all these things by means of which it would seem that the Negro might achieve visibility in American life. But, since none has offered a way into the culture, he has now chosen to become an underground man. All his reversals have been due to the blackness of his skin: so now, at last, he decides to stay in his cellar, where, by way of a tapped line, he will steal the electricity for his 1,369 bulbs from Monopolated Light and Power and dine on sloe gin and vanilla ice cream and *embrace* "The Blackness of Blackness."

Now the descent into "the heart of darkness," as a movement of the spirit, as a way of coming to terms with the self, is at least as old as St. John of the Cross, and actually far older; and it is a stratagem of renewal that has its own dignity and positiveness and moral validity. So Mr. Ellison might very well have simply concluded things at this point, even though to have done so might have been to elicit from secular literati the same irritated puzzlement that T. S. Eliot's reinstatement of the Johannine *askésis* in the *Quartets* had provoked a decade earlier: there was already, in other words, a sufficient positivity in the negativity of that underground room—and *this* wounded Adam, in *deliberately* and *lucidly* making the descent into darkness, was already no longer *merely wounded*, as the author of *The Ascent of Mount Carmel* and *The Dark Night of the Soul* might have certified. But Mr. Ellison was eager to enlist in the "Party of Hope"; so, at the end, he has his hero speaking of his determination "to affirm the principle on which the country was built" and of his intention to play "a socially responsible role." And this is a rhetoric too stilted in tone perhaps to be altogether persuasive.

But the insecurity of vision that seems somewhat to be threatening in the last few pages in no real way invalidates the remarkable poise with which this fine artist has kept his Adam to a course that avoids at once the Scylla of rampant nihilism and the Charybdis of inordinate self-pity. And it is to be hoped that the triumph of art and of moral imagination represented by Mr. Ellison's magnificent book does but pre-

168   sage not only his own future but also the books that are yet to be written by the many gifted young Negro writers who are beginning to appear on the American scene.

NOTES

1. Countee Cullen, "Heritage," in *Anthology of American Negro Literature*, ed. by V. F. Calverton (New York: The Modern Library, 1929), p. 192.

2. *Vide* T. E. Hulme, "Humanism and the Religious Attitude" and "Romanticism and Classicism" in his *Speculations*, ed. Herbert Read (London: Kegan Paul, Trench, Trubner & Co., Ltd., 1936).

3. Randall Stewart, *American Literature and Christian Doctrine* (Baton Rouge: Louisiana State University Press, 1958), p. 55.

4. *Vide* R. W. B. Lewis, "Prologue," *The American Adam: Innocence, Tragedy, and Tradition in the Nineteenth Century* (Chicago: University of Chicago Press, 1959).

5. *Ibid.*, p. 195.

6. *Ibid.*, p. 196.

7. Richard Chase, *The American Novel and Its Tradition* (Garden City: Doubleday Anchor Books, 1957), p. 2.

8. *Ibid.*, p. 4.

9. E. M. Forster, *Aspects of the Novel* (London: Edward Arnold & Co., 1949), p. 134.

10. Leslie Fiedler, *Love and Death in the American Novel* (New York: Criterion Books, 1960), p. 468.

11. Alfred Kazin, "The Stillness of *Light in August*," *Partisan Review*, Vol. XXIV, No. 4 (Fall 1957), p. 533.

12. *Ibid.*, p. 536.

13. Herman Melville, "Hawthorne and His *Mosses*," in *The Shock of Recognition*, ed. Edmund Wilson (Garden City: Doubleday & Co., 1947), p. 192.

14. *Vide* H. Richard Niebuhr, *The Kingdom of God in America* (New York: Harper Torchbooks, 1959).

15. This precise distinction between *what* and *as* is, I think, borrowed from Richard Chase, though I cannot locate just where it is that it is to be found.

16. Richard Chase, *The Democratic Vista* (Garden City: Doubleday Anchor Books, 1958), p. 34.

17. Richard Chase, *The American Novel and Its Tradition*, p. 2.

18. Chase, *The Democratic Vista*, p. 34.

19. *Vide* Edward Shils, "The Culture of the Indian Intellectual," *The*
Sewanee Review, Vol. LXVII, No. 2 (pp. 239–261) and No. 3 (pp. 401–421).

20. James Baldwin, *The Fire Next Time* (New York: Dell, 1964), pp. 44–45.

21. *Ibid.*, p. 61.

22. Lewis, *op. cit.*, pp. 128–129.

23. *Ibid.*, p. 128.

24. *Ibid.*, p. 115.

25. *Ibid.*, p. 132.

26. Charles I. Glicksberg, "Negro Fiction in America," *The South Atlantic Quarterly*, Vol. XLV, No. 4 (October 1946), p. 482.

27. F. W. Dupee, "James Baldwin and the 'Man,'" *The New York Review of Books*, Vol. 1, No. 1 (1963), p. 1.

28. *Vide* Lewis, *op. cit.*, p. 198. Though Professor Lewis's book concentrates on the American nineteenth century, he devotes an "Epilogue" to "The Contemporary Situation," and here he explicitly relates *Invisible Man* to the Emersonian figure.

29. By those familiar with the literature of recent European theology, the phrase "cheap grace" will be recognized as coming from Dietrich Bonhoeffer: *vide* his *The Cost of Discipleship*, trans. R. H. Fuller (New York: Macmillan Co., 1949), Chapter 1.

30. R. W. B. Lewis, "Eccentrics' Pilgrimage" (an omnibus review of Ralph Ellison's *Invisible Man* and several other novels), *The Hudson Review*, Vol. VI, No. 1 (Spring 1953), p. 148.

Death and Transfiguration:
The Lagerkvist Pentalogy

Pär Lagerkvist, the Swedish author and Nobel Prize winner, has crowned his literary career with the recent completion of a pentalogy of novels dealing with man's unending quest for a meaningful life reconciled with a universe of mystery. With the publication of *The Holy Land* (1964), Lagerkvist brought to a close the tale he began in *Barabbas* (1950) and continued in *The Sibyl, The Death of Ahasuerus,* and *Pilgrim at Sea.*

Behind the pentalogy (Lagerkvist's major literary production since World War II) lies, of course, a significant body of preparatory work. Lagerkvist began his career (with the exception of some early social-protest poems) with the publication in 1912 of a romantic narrative called *People,* the inevitable story of a young, sensitive university student, alone in the world and yearning for the real experience of life. But after an eventful trip to Paris in 1913 and an encounter with the French art world, Lagerkvist was awakened to richer, more original, more creative literary possibilities.

Experimenting with drama and verse up through World War I, Lagerkvist first committed himself to the serious philosophical issues that were to be his life's concern in such plays as *The Difficult Hour* (1918) and *The Secret of Heaven* (1919), and in a work of prose fiction, *The Eternal Smile* (1920). Lagerkvist has maintained this commitment ever since and has expressed it in all literary genres—poems, plays, short stories, essays, and novels.

Eschewing naturalism and realism as artistic methods, Lagerkvist developed early in his career an essentially abbreviated and surrealistic literary manner, heavily weighted with symbolism. Although a follower of Strindberg in the drama, Lagerkvist developed in prose a style entirely his own, a style irritatingly succinct to some, but to most readers noteworthy for its provocative brevity, its oblique and suggestive quality, and, above all, its clean, hauntingly simple lines. Lagerkvist is a quiet writer, speaking in a soft, sometimes strange, but always clear voice. He speaks in gentle parables and gentle riddles. He moves the mind more than the heart, yet in some inexplicable way the heart is finally reached.

Lagerkvist, perhaps more than any other twentieth century author, has dealt consistently and artistically with the truly eternal questions: What is the meaning of life? Is there a God? What is death? What is the rationale of existence? What should man be doing? In the course of dealing with those questions, Lagerkvist has moved from an earlier alternation between a joyous, almost ingenuous acceptance of life and a bitter awareness of evil, to a more profound and ambiguous philosophy of pilgrimage and quest. Lagerkvist has more and more described a quest and pilgrimage *away* from that which is totally unacceptable in human experience *toward* states of mind and experience that man can structure for himself in spite of the mysteries and enigmatic forces surrounding him. Always the agnostic, Lagerkvist modified and qualified his agnosticism as the result of the horrors of the Nazi experience in the thirties and forties; and in the fifties he emerged a more complex, but no less controlled or compelling, metaphysician than before.

And it is as a literary metaphysician, as a religiously oriented writer, that Lagerkvist has written, in the pentalogy beginning with *Barabbas*, a slender but provocative myth of resurrection. Writing in a century in which cultures, nations, and people have survived vast physical destruction, in a century in which the death of six million can be followed by rebirth into nation and state, Lagerkvist explores the very meaning of *thanatos* and escape from *thanatos*, not simply on the ordinary level of flesh but on the more refined level of spirit, not simply in the ordinary terms of personal or corporate existence but in the greater terms of transfiguration.

Lagerkvist's pentalogy is, quite simply, a challenge to the secular, rational evaluation of survival, a challenge to a modern world dedicated to, and increasingly skillful in, survival techniques—miracle drugs and heart transplants—yet faced with the problem of properly using the survival it manages to achieve. Lagerkvist challenges that same over-evaluation of survival that was satirized in the famous conversation between Voltaire's Micromegas and the Saturnian, wherein the Saturnian explains that his people live normally some 15,000 years—though "that is no better than dying almost as soon as a person is born." Even if man survives almost forever, he still hungers for more: "Our life is a simple little dot, our existence a flash, our planet an atom. Scarcely has a person begun to improve himself than death comes."

Obviously, for Lagerkvist—and for Voltaire—survival is not enough; there is never *enough* survival to make survival worthwhile. Stretch out human life as far as one will, increase the longevity of the individual existence, and the goal of real life is not necessarily achieved. No matter how far one stretches the boundaries of mortal existence, one has not necessarily solved the problem of human life, its meaning and its significance. Lagerkvist therefore must bring us to his simple question: Is there some way man can move from the limited

174   miracle of physical survival to a greater miracle of spiritual transformation?

II

One of the principal literary devices used by Lagerkvist in his study of death and transfiguration is the Lazarus archetype, the man returned from the dead to the realities of this world. To a certain extent, the entire pentalogy is a study of the Lazarus figure, not simply the prototypal Lazarus who appears in *Barabbas*, the first novel of the series, but the various Lazarus figures who are the main characters in all the novels.

Lazarus, in the pentalogy, is the representation of the living-dead—and hence is the representation of modern man. Displacing the orthodox concept of Lazarus as the fortunate man snatched from the jaws of death, Lagerkvist presents, rather, a Lazarus who is victim of survival, the man dragged back into existence to dramatize the very meaninglessness of that existence. Lazarus lives on his mountainside outside Bethany, lives alone and alienated from his society, lives on bread and salt, cares nothing for anyone or any event, is the perfectly disengaged and ultimately estranged human being. Lagerkvist's depiction of a melancholy and passive Lazarus emphasizes two of Lagerkvist's observations of the human condition: the intolerableness of simple existence and the over-evaluation of that existence by mankind at large; Lazarus knows the "nothingness" of his survival, but the Christian community assumes that his survival is his most precious gift, indeed a divine reward and blessing.

And Lagerkvist's depiction of a hollow-spirited Lazarus is his most radical demonstration in the pentalogy that death and resurrection must be more than physical events, more than a dying to the physical world followed only by a rebirth into the world, that death and resurrection must finally be events of a higher and different order—if modern man genuinely desires any sort of meaningful accommodation to the eternal mysteries that confront him, or if he genuinely desires his days to be more than a dull and paralyzing stretch of time.

Lagerkvist's Lazarus-truth is further dramatized in the pentalogy by a number of other survival heroes, all of whom have similar experiences of "dying" and escaping from their "deaths" back into an inadequate world. Barabbas, with whom the pentalogy begins, is—in an exchange with Christ—saved from the death-like existence of his prison-grave and is returned to existence in Jerusalem, only to find that he, like Lazarus, is confronted with meaninglessness. His friend the fat lady explains, "If a man is sentenced to death then he's dead, and if he's let out and reprieved, he's still dead, because that's what he's been and he is only risen again from the dead, and that's not the same as living. . . ."

Barabbas finds no joy in his recovered life, can only act out the tawdry role of contemporary man: he hurls himself into sensuality, thievery, murder in a desperate struggle for meaning, only to remain forever disillusioned and spiritually confused. And more than once he acts out the ersatz death-and-resurrection of modern man: He is buried in the grave of the Roman copper mines as a slave; he is resurrected into the dull, pointless routine of serving a Roman master. He "dies" into the confusion of the labyrinthine catacombs of Rome; he is "resurrected" into a night filled with darkness and deception. Yet we are told that he always had death "inside him, he had had that inside him as long as he had lived." Barabbas, modern man, is "immured in himself, in his own realm of death."

Ahasuerus, the wandering Jew (appearing in *The Sibyl* and *The Death of Ahasuerus*) is also burdened with survival. Having refused to let Christ, on the way to the cross, rest against his wall, Ahasuerus is cursed with eternal life, eternal survival, and becomes a haunted man. Given pure, unadulterated absolute survival, he loses the essence of life—he loses wife and child, he loses identity, he loses community, he loses pleasure, he loses his humanity. "Had it not always been my dearest wish never to have to die? . . . Why then did I not rejoice? Why did I feel no gladness?"

And there are others: Tobias, in *The Death of Ahasuerus*, *Pilgrim at Sea*, and *The Holy Land*, is the man who has survived the wars and the social upheavals of his day, whose life is saved when Diana, the woman who loves him, steps in front of the murderous arrow meant for him. Giovanni, in *Pilgrim at Sea* and *The Holy Land*, has survived his own violation of the codes and taboos of an ordered civilization and survives the brutal world of the pirate ship. Yet all of Lagerkvist's survival heroes are unhappy and alienated men—they survive, but they are sullen, staring, antisocial men, living on their own Lazarus forms of bread and salt, increasingly unconcerned with the world and its nothingness. All of Lagerkvist's survival heroes are frustrated and confused, burdened with their own spiritual emptiness.

The inadequacy of simple survival is underlined by Lagerkvist in his use of two supernatural events—the resurrection of Christ from the tomb and the assumption of the god Apollo from Mount Parnassus. Lagerkvist uses Christ and Apollo—not in any literal acceptance of their supernatural nature—but as literary symbols to disqualify any less magnificent form of survival in this world. In *Barabbas*, Christ ascends from his rocky grave, and in *The Sibyl*, Apollo escapes from this world on a cold winter's night back into the mysterious regions of his deity. Both events are demonstrations of what man's easy, too-available survival simply is not. Lagerkvist uses the mythic tales of Christ and Apollo to make certain the contrast with all the Lazarus resurrections that human beings settle for. In the myths of Christ and Apollo, the resurrections are "out of this world," the escape from death is into a new dimension—and though man may not be expected to achieve the miracle of the gods, man need not settle either for the ordinarily human. Christ and Apollo are used by Lagerkvist to

remind us that man must not be saved simply for a renewed
ordinary perception, but must be saved out of that perception
into new realms of life, beyond the grave of living-death that
the contemporary secular world inevitably is.

III

With Lazarus on the one hand, Christ and Apollo on the
other, Lagerkvist moves to the question, Can man progress
from one nature to another? He presents his discussion of
hoped-for transfiguration in a myth of perception. He develops
at length, in the pentalogy, the dilemma of modern man in
terms of his capacity to see—although limited vision is typical
of all his survival heroes. Lazarus is described as "sitting . . .
gazing straight out into the room . . . He seemed not to notice
them" with his "pale, lack-lustre eyes . . . queer, opaque eyes
that expressed nothing at all." The condition of the eyes for
Lagerkvist is the condition of the soul, seeing but not seeing,
living but not living.

The discussion of man's inner vision in terms of man's real
eyesight is not new in literature, of course. Tiresias says to
Oedipus that, in effect, he has eyes but cannot see, and in a
more modern literature, T. S. Eliot, discussing the same contemporary condition that Lagerkvist is analyzing, says that
the modern hollow man, surviving in the dead land, is "Sight-
less, unless/The eyes reappear," and dwells in a condition
wherein "The eyes are not here. . . ."

Barabbas, perhaps Lagerkvist's most complete presentation
of secular man, has "eye-sockets expressionless." And the first
mention of Barabbas, at the very beginning of the pentalogy,
is that he was "a man standing with his eyes riveted" on the
crucified Christ. Lagerkvist declares at once that his tale is a
tale of perception, and he also declares that Barabbas—the
survival hero—has "eyes too deep-set, as though they wanted
to hide."

178   Looking upon the world with eyes that want to hide, or with Eliot's eyes that are not here, can Lazarus-man see the Christ or the Apollo? Lagerkvist suggests that secular modern man does have within him the capacity to envision the signs of inner transfiguration, to see the possibility of transformation within himself—but man denies his own vision, rejects what is apparent before him. Looking at the dying Christ, Barabbas *thinks* (and where else but in our thinking does our transformation begin or end?) that the Christ is "surrounded by a dazzling light." But his own reaction to his "first glance," his own intuitive realization of transfiguration, is to rationalize the dazzling light: "It must have been because he came straight from the dungeon and his eyes were still unused to the glare .... Soon afterwards the light vanished ... and his sight grew normal again."

And later, when he speaks to his fellow criminals about the darkness-at-noon that fell upon Golgotha, he again denies his vision, accepts the reasonable explanations of a reasonable, secular world: "It must be because there was something wrong with his eyes. ... The fat woman said that of course it must be due to that, the fact that his eyes had not got used to the light, that he had been blinded by the light for awhile."

Yet Barabbas, torn between desire for a transfiguring vision and desire for a comforting blindness, is haunted by the problem of his eyes: "Perhaps something had gone wrong with them during his time in prison?" When he is confronted with the ultimate sign of transfiguration, when he has the choice to make—to see or not to see—he stares, Lazarus-like, true survival-hero, upon the event of blinding light and Christ's emptied tomb and sees nothing, sees nothing and rejoices: "Deep down inside he thought how very pleased he was not to have seen it. It showed that his eyes were all right now, like everybody else's eyes, that he no longer saw any vision but only reality itself." While the hare-lip girl, also a witness at the resurrection, has "eyes radiant with the memory of what

she had seen," Barabbas rejoices at his spiritual blindness—
and his normality.

The denial of vision is not, however, easy for man. Barabbas
is burdened with the knowledge that others do "see." The
hare-lip girl's last words in life are, "I see Him. I see Him."
And Sahak, Barabbas's fellow prisoner in the copper mines, is
resurrected from the depths, not to an ordinary world but a
world that causes the slave to cry, "He has come! He has come!
Behold, his kingdom is here!" And at life's end, when Barabbas
wanders in the maze of the catacombs, glimpsing a distant
light—the distant light of that "other world" into which true
resurrections take us, "He put his hand to his head. To his
eyes. Whatever kind of light was it he had seen? Wasn't it
a light? Was it only imagination, or something funny with
his eyes? . . ."

If Lagerkvist had ended his myth of death and resurrection
with the story of Barabbas, we would have a striking denun-
ciation of secular man and a great expression of the denial
of vision and what vision symbolizes: man's transformed
situation. But Lagerkvist pursued the matter further and
brought his myth to a more hopeful conclusion.

The wandering Jew, Ahasuerus, is also a survival hero and
like his companions in secular existence, "would often stand
staring in front of me, or out of the window, with empty eyes,
seeing nothing. . . ." Yet Ahasuerus is different from Barabbas,
for Ahasuerus, when confronted with the miraculous ascension
of Apollo ("Now he has thrown off the garments in which he
hid, his earthly husk, and became again what he really was")
does not deny what he has seen, but accepts his vision as valid,
and allows himself to begin the progress from one world to
another within his own identity.

The progress is not easy. It is not instantaneous. But
Ahasuerus moves in the direction of Lagerkvist's holy land,
and comes at last to the escape from mere survival and existence. His own real death is evidence, within the terms of

180   his particular myth, that his Lazarus days are over, that he
has come to that new vision, that transformation, that will
allow him to step out of the Lazarus-world into another state
of being. Lying in the monastery bed, Ahasuerus realizes that
"He must be in a kind of swoon—a swoon of light." He is a
new man: "All at once the room was filled with light. It was
extraordinary. And it happened suddenly as by a miracle.
'What's this light—this glorious light I can see?'"

Ahasuerus has come to the beatific vision—not a vision *of*
another world (the light he sees is simply the sunlight shining
through the window), but a vision *in* another world. He now
can *see* the sunlight as he had never seen it before, and so seeing it, he himself is in a new world, is truly resurrected into
a new dimension of life.

IV

Barabbas fails. Ahasuerus succeeds. Lazarus remains Lazarus, or he enacts within himself the "spiritual ascension" of
Christ and Apollo. Modern man is presented with the choice
of emulating one or another, although Lagerkvist does not
suggest that man will inevitably do so. Not everyone in
Lagerkvist's novels reaches a holy land, but some do, and that
is the hopeful aspect of Lagerkvist's moral essay. It leads
Lagerkvist to a consideration of the nature of the holy land,
the nature of "spiritual ascension within," to a consideration
of the quality of our vision, and the modes of our perception
that identify our transformations.

In the last two novels of the pentalogy, *Pilgrim at Sea* and
The Holy Land, Lagerkvist accompanies two more representa-
tives of contemporary man—Giovanni and Tobias—on their
journey to the holy land, where they do achieve transfiguration
prior to their physical deaths. Tobias, a man in the turmoil of
postwar existence, has, like Barabbas and Ahasuerus, had his
opportunity to know about transformation: he has seen in the

ravaged village a dead woman with the sign of the stigmata upon her, and this is his epiphany. Death, but a miracle upon it. More like Ahasuerus than Barabbas, he responds to the epiphany and does not deny his having seen it. Moved by this "sudden glimpse" he struggles to achieve the complete escape from blindness, the true awakening, that he can anticipate. Joining with Giovanni on the pilgrim ship, he comes at last to the holy land where the final stages of his true perception are to occur.

For Lagerkvist, the holy land is the land of potential symbols. It is a haunting landscape: ruined temple, simple herdsmen, divine baby, snake-woman, three crosses, river of death, white goddess. All these artifacts are spread out before Tobias and Giovanni in what is the manifestation of that final and ultimate state of mind wherein man encounters the basic realities, freed from the blindness of secularism. Giovanni comes to the holy land literally a blind man, yet he comes, we are told, with "better knowledge"; though his eyes are now "empty and expressionless," they are at least not falsely open, pretending to see while not seeing, as do the eyes of Lazarus and Barabbas. Indeed, Giovanni, blind to the secular world, now "sees" a symbolic world, the world that we create in our minds or, in a Platonic sense, discover in the heights of our minds where our "spiritual ascension" has taken us.

Lagerkvist's holy land is the same holy land that Rilke urges upon us when, in the *Duino Elegies, IX*, he speaks of an invisible earth ascending in us; when he asks the Earth if its imperative to us is not indeed "transformation." Lagerkvist's holy land—the final place of vision, the place where we truly see—is cerebral and archetypal, a psychologic *aftonland*, that condition wherein man, in his own creative capacity, walks through a transfigured state of being. Lagerkvist's holy land is one that frequently begins, as it did for Ahasuerus, in the experience upon Mount Parnassus—that mountain of poetry and art and creativity.

Indeed, as Lagerkvist has written and published the novels of his pentalogy, it has been increasingly evident that he himself, in his art, has been moving from a literal level maintained rather consistently in *Barabbas*, to a symbolic level hinted at in *The Sibyl*, and brought closer to the surface in *The Death of Ahasuerus* and *Pilgrim at Sea*. In *The Holy Land* the ascension of the symbolic is completed.

It is from the perspective of this total symbolism of *The Holy Land* that we see the solution to the problem of Giovanni's empty locket: perhaps the crucial problem in our comprehension of Lagerkvist's message about human life.

Long ago, as a young man, Giovanni had taken from the woman he loved a locket, a locket without a picture in it but which, nevertheless, Giovanni kept all his life. It has become for him a symbol—and like all symbols it need not be something literal within itself. Its entire value as a symbol is that it has meaning, rather than content. It is an object which Giovanni himself invests with meaning. Lagerkvist would seem to suggest that all "things" are empty in essence: that even such a thing as the Eucharist, for instance, though demonstrated to be scientifically empty, may yet function in the religious life because it has meaning. Lagerkvist would seem to suggest that indeed all the artifacts of this world, all objects and persons and events are, in the holy land of the transformed mind, the potential recipients of our investment, and that it is by our investments that we achieve our new world, our new life.

It would be wrong, however, to read Lagerkvist as a traditional Transcendentalist. He is not suggesting that transformed man now has the visionary capacity to read *through* a secular world into a supernatural truth. Rather, transformed man has the visionary capacity to see new meaning in this world, to find in the secular world, with all its physical and material manifestations, what the visionary poet Walt Whitman also found in the tangible things he called "you dumb, beautiful ministers." They are ministers in that they reflect

upon us whatever visionary light we cast upon them from
within ourselves.

Tobias, the last of Lagerkvist's survival heroes, a man who
begins as a Lazarus but who is able by inner will to come to
vision, walks up and through the mountains of the holy land,
at the pentalogy's conclusion, encountering the signs, artifacts,
and archetypes that confront all men in the journey of life.
He confronts them in their nudity, their expectancy. He finds
the three crosses upon Calvary—but they are empty crosses.
They are to mean whatever man would have them mean. They
are not messages waiting to be read; they are tablets upon
which man is to write. If a man is transformed, if he is more
than Lazarus and Barabbas, he will write the message that will
make his life meaningful. Tobias is able to do that, and by so
doing he reconciles all the loose ends of his life, transforms
all the old "blood memories" of ancient loves and ancient
guilt into penance and salvation. He can end his life "full of
great peace."

Lagerkvist's pentalogy thus concludes with a magnificently
effective "acting out" of an ultimate state of mind that—for the
Christian humanist that Lagerkvist finally is—represents the
holy land of accommodation to life, an accommodation
achieved by escaping our Lazarus existence and seeing life
truly from the perspective of spiritual resurrection, "in this
world but not of it," touching with our minds those
transcendental and archetypal realities that are knowable
beneath and above the secular glare, and seeing all things of
this world with new eyes, with eyes truly open, making their
investment in the nature of things.

Lagerkvist believes certainly in dying to this world and in
being reborn. But he questions always a rebirth into the same
limited mind and perspective. He finds modern man, blind
and groping, quite the master of existence, but not the master
of life. He calls for modern man to open his eyes into a creative vision that will transform the world in front of him.

Lagerkvist goes no farther than that. He takes his survival heroes to their real and physical death, but he does not step over into the question of immortality or eternity. He neither accepts nor rejects the metanatural possibilities. He remains ambiguous about things beyond our time and our space. Lagerkvist believes in God—but the divine is forever *deus absconditus*. What concerns Lagerkvist primarily is the achievement of a spiritual life here and now, the achievement of a spiritual life that will permit us to come to real death with peace and serenity, that will permit us to die saying that we have truly lived.

All in all, Lagerkvist offers one of the great spiritual challenges of modern literature. He challenges man to a spiritual perception of life. In so doing, he is hopeful without being sentimental. He avoids the pitfall of seeking final answers, and he speaks tellingly and profoundly to a disturbed, myopic, and anxious world.

BIBLIOGRAPHY

Lagerkvist, Pär. *Barabbas*, trans. Alan Blair (New York: Random House, 1951).

———. *The Sibyl*, trans. Naomi Walford (New York: Random House, 1958).

———. *The Death of Ahasuerus*, trans. Naomi Walford (New York: Random House, 1962).

———. *Pilgrim at Sea*, trans. Naomi Walford (New York: Random House, 1964).

———. *The Holy Land*, trans. Naomi Walford (New York: Random House, 1966).

Ahnebrink, Lars. "Pär Lagerkvist: A Seeker and a Humanist," *Pacific Spectator*, VI (1952), 400–412.

Spector, Robert D. "Lagerkvist and Existentialism," *Scandinavian Studies*, XXXII (1960), 203–211.

"They That Have Not Heard Shall Understand": A Study of Heinrich Böll

Heinrich Böll often lets his better nature get the worst of him. Many of the elements in his early work now seem rather sentimental: the lonely figure of the *Landser*, the ordinary soldier, a mere pawn overwhelmed by events on the front and stumbling uncomprehendingly and without protest toward an absurd, useless, and inevitable death; the omnipresent railway stations through which people pass on their way to the front or on their return to obliterated homes without ever meeting each other (an eager critic wrote of Böll's *ferroviarischem Symbolismus*); the consistent use of flashback techniques which evoke a wistful nostalgia for an orderly, though already hypocritical, world before the war; internal monologues by the main characters, consecutive but rarely converging, thus heightening our awareness that the essential human condition is solitary introspection, not solidarity; and everywhere the orphans and victimized children. Joining with these better impulses is a fine sense of the ridiculous: the music-loving concentration camp commander, *Obersturmführer* Filskeit, who grants a stay of execution to those prisoners who can enrich the camp choir, and provisionally ignores the principles of his own prize-winning monograph on "the relationship between race and choir." Böll's comment on Dickens' sense of humor seems a perfect self-definition: "Dickens' eye was always a little moist, and the Latin word for moisture is *Humor*."

Back in the 1950's, when Böll's first novels and tales appeared in English some five years or so after their publication in German, his apparent sentimentality constituted a good measure of his attraction. We were relieved, I suppose, that George Steiner, in his role as the Cassandra of the death of German literary language, was being undercut by a talent as impressive as Böll's, though one wondered in those depressingly dynamic days of German economic recovery whether the writers in their Volkswagens had forgotten the war and the concentration camps as quickly as the industrialists in their Mercedes. The Gruppe 47 had not yet visited Princeton, of course; Günter Grass had not yet been translated. In short, despite "Literary Letters from Europe" in the *Sunday Times Book Review*, we were pretty ignorant. Was there literary material in the horror, or merely superlative statistics for sociologists and for fellowships of reconciliation? Böll's early works provided a welcome tentative answer. His melody was pure; his mode understatement; his style apparently sparse and factual. He was attractive too because he was a Catholic who, despite the war, did not seem to believe in the Apocalypse: he was compassionate rather than visionary. He was perhaps overly fond of his own characters and, implicitly, a bit self-indulgent; he had not yet shaken off that Rhineland sweetness which was later to annoy him so.

Heinrich Böll has a keen sense of the symbolic power of emblematic epigraphs and quotations. *Und sagte kein einziges Wort*, his 1953 novel attacking religious hypocrisy, has a title which communicates the essence of his Christian vision: "He never said a mumblin' word," sings a Negro. The title is

simply a German translation of the refrain from the spiritual
(Richard Graves has insensitively given the English version the
unfortunate title *Acquainted with the Night*). "They nailed
Him to the Cross, and He never said a word." Christ is the
victim, He is overwhelmed by hostile forces, He does not protest His fate, He cannot even understand it—the cry "*Lamma,
Lamma, Sabachthani*" implies a metaphysic beyond the concept of Christ found in the simple spiritual. For the Böll of the
novels and stories of the early 1950's, the victims, whether
they be foot soldiers or civilians, are Christ; and the execu-
tioners are the powerful of the earth, the officers, the industrialists, the Pharisees. As with Dostoevsky, one can often
measure in Böll the saintliness of a character by the extent of
his silences. The hangmen are articulate; Christ "never said
a mumblin' word."

   This pattern is made amply clear in the brilliant story,
"Murke's Collected Silences," first published in the *Frank-
furter Hefte* in 1955. Murke, a *cum laude* graduate in psychology, works in the ultramodern Broadcasting House, where his
existential morning prayer consists of riding through the locks
of the paternoster lift, "open cages carried on a conveyor belt,
like beads on a rosary, . . . so that passengers could step on and
off at any floor." Murke's pressing assignment in the Cultural
Department is to re-edit two talks on *The Nature of Art* by the
great Professor Bur-Malottke, who had converted to Catholicism during the religious fervor of the guilt-ridden year 1945,
but who had deconverted suddenly. In the two talks "God"
occurs twenty-seven times, and it is the Professor's intention
to cut "God" out of the tapes and to replace Him with "the
higher Being Whom we revere." That Murke, despite his degree in psychology, is the only Christian in the story, becomes
apparent not only in the antipathy he feels toward Bur-
Malottke, the go-getting opportunist caricatured in so many of
Böll's works, but in two symbolic passages.

   From his mother Murke had received a tawdry, highly

colored print of the Sacred Heart with the words "I prayed for you at St. James Church." Instead of throwing out that sentimental card, he decides, in irritation at the "impressive rugs, the impressive corridors, the impressive furniture, and the pictures in excellent taste," to establish the Sacred Heart in the impeccable surroundings of Broadcasting House by sticking it on the office door of the Assistant Drama Producer: "Thank God, now there's at least one corny picture in this place." The second passage involves Murke's extraordinary hobby. Against all network regulations, he collects leftover snips of tape: " 'When I have to cut tapes, in the places where the speakers sometimes pause for a moment—or sigh, or take a breath, or there is absolute silence—I don't throw that away. I collect it. Incidentally, there wasn't a single second of silence in Bur-Malottke's tapes.' " And in the evenings he splices the silences together and plays them to himself: "I have only three minutes so far—but then people aren't silent very often."

A perverse kind of *deus ex machina* brings the two strains together. The Assistant Drama Producer decides to revise an edifying radio play about an atheist who taunts God with questions and is answered only by silence. Twelve of Bur-Malottke's excised "God's" will replace the silences. "You really are a godsend," the Assistant Producer says to the technician who offers the snippets from Murke's tin collection box. And Murke now will be able to add almost a full minute of silence to his nightly tape-recorded prayers. The intimation here is that a real God is in those silences; the rest is sham. But the reader wonders whether that tawdry card with its inscription, "I prayed for you at St. James Church," did not also have some mystical effect on the Assistant Drama Producer, causing him to revise his radio play.

"One must pray in order to console God," the Jewess Ilona in *Adam, Where Art Thou?* had told the taciturn foot soldier Feinhals. One of Böll's most attractive qualities as a Catholic novelist is that he finds Christ more often than not among the non-Christians and the unbelievers. It is Ilona who auditions for the concentration camp choir with the All Saints Litany and who instead of appealing to the music-loving commandant with her angelic voice arouses in him such a sexual paroxysm of raging impotence and guilt that he shoots her. Pilate has done his job again. But Ilona's words live on in the former architect who had kissed her once under the trees before returning to the front. He will pray to console God for the faces and sermons of the priests, Feinhals thinks shortly before his pathetic death at the very doorstep of his home.

Among the most important currents in Böll's work, and one which links it to so much Catholic imaginative writing of our time, is his relentless caricaturing of the Pharisees. Truly, God needs consoling when faced with some of the faithful in *Acquainted with the Night*. Mrs. Franke, a powerful force in diocesan intrigues, pronounces the word "money" with a tenderness which appalls, using just the intonation with which others might pronounce "life, love, death, or God." Her work in the parish amounts to little more than trading "in the most precious of all commodities, in God." Even her domestic chores become reflections of her religiosity; she counts her preserve jars "as if she were gently chanting the cadences of some secret liturgy." In contrast, Böll presents us with two of his most touching characters, Fred and Kate, who would doubtless be castigated as sinners by a Mrs. Franke. Fred, whose father was an ex-priest, has left Kate out of self-hatred and now sleeps in the railway station, drinking heavily but sending what little money he has to his impoverished wife. They meet as guilt-ridden "lovers" in a sordid hotel room: "It is terrible to love and to be married."

As a social document, *Acquainted with the Night* might be read as a protest against poverty amid prosperity, or even as a treatise on the consequences of the postwar housing shortage. But it is, above all, a religious novel. Fred and Kate are among those who are crucified in silence. It is she who hears the Negro singing his plaintive spiritual. When Kate finally summons up enough nerve to go to a confessional, she sees the priest watching the clock and in anger protests against "the clergy who lived in great houses and had faces like advertisements for complexion cream." Through Fred's eyes we see the hypocrisy of the postwar religious revival. Even a druggists' convention requires ecclesiastical collaboration. Amid signs proclaiming "Trust your Druggist" and balloons advertising toothpaste (one company actually drops tubes of dentifrice on the crowd) march the clergy; the bishop himself, apparently falling into an instinctive goosestep, heads the procession. But despite the venality, or perhaps because of it, the Host remains pristine, and Fred cannot resist kneeling and crossing himself: "For a moment I had the feeling of being a hypocrite until it came to my mind that God was not to blame for the inadequacies of His servants and that it was no hypocrisy to kneel before Him."

Unlike so many Catholic novelists of our time (Bernanos, Langgässer, Graham Greene), Böll is refreshingly free from dualism. For him, the way to God does not necessarily lead first to Satan. Nor, however, does it lead to conventional orthodoxy. Fred Bogner is a true Christian; he sees through cant and understands the true mystical impulse. He sympathizes with a priest who has become unpopular (achieving only a delta-plus on his evaluation card) because his sermons were not sentimental enough for his parishioners' operetta tastes. He recognizes, in a strange vision of a holy family, the sincerity of a pretty girl whose idiot brother, while frightened of trams, is transformed by the singing of the monks.

That Fred's naive and instinctive mysticism is for him an ideal can be seen in the conclusion of an early Böll story, "Candles for Maria" (1950). Electricity has made candles obsolete, and an apparently callous candle manufacturer tries unsuccessfully to dispose of his now useless merchandise to a wholesaler in religious goods. Having missed his train, he follows a young couple into a church, tries to pray, confesses himself, and finally converts his very merchandise into prayer by lighting all the candles from his suitcase at the altar. "My heart felt happier than it ever had before," he is able to say at last.

In his *Letter to a Young Catholic*, Böll directly attacks the Church for its preoccupation with such superficial questions as determining what kinds of print and paper are most suitable for army prayerbooks. He cautions a prospective draftee against the new "gym-teacher's theology." Elsewhere, he warns writers against winking knowingly at their public. Almost all of his works with a postwar setting contribute to the current of anti-Pharisee humor initiated by *Acquainted with the Night*. (Böll himself succumbs to the Catholic in-jokes he derided in a memorable, untranslatable phrase as *das Konfekt der Eingeweihten*.) Bertha, in the story "Like a Bad Dream," had learned from the nuns at boarding school that her husband should wear a dark jacket and conservative tie to consummate an important business deal. Did the nuns teach her to know instinctively that her husband would have to offer a large bribe to win the contract, or that the best way to lure a colleague into an adjoining room to talk business was to suggest that he might be interested in seeing an eighteenth century crucifix hanging in that room? And yet it is she who in reaction to her husband's expletive, "Christ, it means 20,000 marks to me," answers: "One should never mention Christ's name in connection with money." Forceful and indignant when a man named Fink confesses his adultery with a married housewife, the priest in "The Adventure" changes his tone upon hearing that the houses which Fink sells are not quite the way they look in the catalogue: "The priest could not suppress an 'Aha.' He said: 'We must be honest about that too, although . . .' he groped for words, 'although it seems impossible. But it is a lie to sell something of whose value one is not convinced.'" Those are double-edged words which conclude the priest's admonition. Fink is weary and unable to pray until through half-closed, sleepy lids he sees a symbol of naive faith, the silhouette of a small old woman outlined in gigantic detail on the wall of the center nave: "a childlike nose and the tired slackness of her lips moving silently: a fleeting memorial, towering above the truncated plaster figures and seeming to grow out beyond the edge of the roof."

Even in his recent novel, *The Clown* (1963), Böll remains true to this satiric pattern in his savage attack on the "Group of Progressive Catholics" who seem, in the eyes of the clown, "to be crocheting themselves loincloths out of Thomas Aquinas, St. Francis of Assisi, Bonaventure and Pope Leo XIII, loincloths which of course failed to cover their nakedness, for . . . there was no one there who wasn't earning at least fifteen hundred marks a month." There are only four Catholics in the world, we are repeatedly told: Pope John, Alec Guinness, Marie (the clown's mistress), and Gregory, an old Negro boxer now earning a meager living as a strong man in vaudeville. When Marie yields at last to the blandishments of Prelate Sommerwild and his fashionable Catholics, she is castigated by her ex-lover as a new first lady of German Catholicism, another Jacqueline Kennedy! Even the clown's own brother, Leo, is unable to help, for the monks whom Leo has joined are apparently always in the refectory eating cabbage or deserts. "If our era deserves a name, it would have to be called the era of prostitution," the clown concludes.

The third emblematic quotation I have chosen to evoke an essential aspect of Böll's novelistic vision serves as epigraph, and contributes the title, to one of his earliest efforts, *Adam, Where Art Thou?* It is taken from the 1940 *Tag- und Nachtbücher* of Theodore Haecker, and reads in full as follows: "A world catastrophe can be of great service. It can also serve as an alibi before God. 'Adam, where wert thou?' 'I was in the world war.' " For Germans of Böll's generation, the war was the central existential event, separating the few who retained

their integrity from the many who gave in to "bad faith" (in
the Sartrian sense). Böll himself served on several fronts and
was wounded in action; he will clearly not be one of those
Romantics who glory in their fictitious role in an imaginary
German Resistance. Nor will he offer breast-beating novels
of remorse to assuage the consciences of his complacent compatriots. He accepts the incontrovertible necessity of service
in the Wehrmacht, but asks implicitly, "What *kind* of a soldier?" And he has far less sympathy for those on the home
front making money than for the *Landser* shooting blindly at
a faceless enemy. It would appear that in his works with a
war setting, Böll often takes at face value Haecker's ironic remark on catastrophe serving as an alibi before God, but that
were he to apply this epigraph to his most recent works, *Billiards at Half-Past Nine* and *The Clown*, he would emphasize
the irony.

Böll quotes as a second epigraph to *Adam, Where Art Thou?*
Saint-Exupéry's *locus classicus* that war is a disease exactly
like typhoid. Yet Böll, curiously enough, does not take very
seriously, at least in his earlier works, his role as diagnostician.
He neither describes the causes of infection nor offers prescrip-
tions for a cure or a preventive. Though most of the *Landser*
we meet in *The Train Was on Time* (1949) and *Adam, Where
Art Thou?* are Catholics by birth, Böll never burdens his war
novels with the recondite religious symbolism which crushed
Elisabeth Langgässer's *The Quest* and *The Indelible Seal*. Re-
trospectively, however, we can feel that the image of the crucifixion conveyed in the words of the Negro spiritual would
apply to his vision of the war:

A crowd of infantry men and pioneers who seemed very
tired were squatting near a barn and many of them lay on the
ground smoking. Then they came to a town and on leaving it
the man in the lookout heard shots for the first time. A heavy
battery was firing from the right of the road. Huge barrels pointed
steeply into the air, black against the dark blue sky. Blood-red

fire spurted from the muzzles and cast a soft red reflection on the wall of a barn. The man ducked: he had never heard any shooting before and now he was frightened. He suffered from ulcers—very serious ulcers.

In this passage the author seems objective and neutral, writing in accordance with the famous *neue Sachlichkeit*. The colors are exploited mainly for chromatic contrast (black, then dark blue, then blood-red to soft red), but they also mirror human emotions, although this is never made explicit by any direct links between characters and colors. (One might say that the progression of colors corresponds with the soldier's reactions to gunfire, which run from apathy to fear to apprehensive resignation.) The plastic contours offer yet another contrast: the squatting men, the angular projections of the steeply pointing barrels, the blurred outlines of a color reflected on the wall of a barn. Despite the appearance of objectivity, this passage from *Adam, Where Art Thou?* represents what I consider the sentimentality of Böll's war narratives. He tells us simply enough that the lookout had never heard shots before, that he ducked and was frightened. This description nonetheless creates a bond of sympathy between reader and character, a bond heightened by the revelation, still factual in tone, that the lookout had ulcers, very serious ulcers. From the crowd of soldiers squatting and smoking, a detail which leaves us emotionally indifferent, we move to the individual, a nervous worrier who is inexperienced, frightened, and tormented with ulcers. Here is another victim about to be crucified by the hostile forces of "heavy batteries," "huge barrels," and "blood-red fire." The lookout somehow seems terribly small; he does not protest, he only worries.

The plot of *Adam, Where Art Thou?* is typical of those found in Böll's novels through *Billiards at Half-Past Nine*, in that fragments of different lives are narrated sequentially, brought together in momentary convergence, then dispersed again: solitude is the human predicament. Despite the large cast of characters in a very short book, the plot is basically simple, alternating between portraits and descriptions of soldiers *en situation*. Böll's double postulation of caricature and sentimental compassion is everywhere apparent. Thus, we have the Nazi Dr. Greck, a violent anti-Semite, contrasted with the helpless architect Feinhals and the Jewess Ilona: "You're like wolves that at any moment can begin to love," she says of the foot soldier. Too often, it seems to me, Böll structures his plot to evoke the maximum of pathos: the battle casualty, Captain Bauer, whose wife after many miscarriages got cancer, mysteriously whispers "Bjeljogorsche" every fifty seconds, recalling Kurtz's repetition of "the horror . . ."; the innkeeper Finck, ordered to procure a case of Tokay wine, is shot by a sniper while protecting his suitcase filled with the precious bottles; and when Feinhals has paid his visit of condolence to Finck's family in the neighboring village of Weidesheim and is in sight of his own home, he is struck down by a shell. The white tablecloth that his family had hung on the outside of their house to signify their surrender to the Allies falls on Feinhals: a final shroud of purity, another silent death.

II

"I had always wanted to write, I tried my hand at it early, but it was only later that I found the right words," Böll wrote in a brief autobiographical essay, "Über mich selbst," in 1958. His most recent novels to be translated into English, *Billiards at Half-Past Nine* (1959) and *The Clown* (1963), are Böll's most ambitious works, both thematically and technically, and they deserve detailed, individual treatment here. Better than any of his earlier creations, these two novels communicate what is noblest and most original in Böll's Catholic vision.

The central event in *Billiards* is the eightieth birthday celebration of Heinrich Faehmel, the patriarch of a family now in its third generation in Bonn. Such an event is always a time for memories and self-appraisal, and this novel exists in the present through dialogue and in many fragments of the past through a complex network of internal monologues and leit-motifs owing more to Virginia Woolf and to *le nouveau roman* than to Faulkner or Joyce. The point of view in the novel is constantly shifting, often without real justification, and since the fête brings together all living members of this once large family, as well as coincidentally some outsiders who once played important roles in their lives, almost everyone is given extensive internal monologues. One of the failings of this perhaps too complicated book is that these many monologues are not sufficiently individualized for the reader to grasp that the point of view (there are no real transitions) has once again changed. Be that as it may, what Böll clearly intends is for this family and its acquaintances to represent Germany and for the constant summoning up of the past to afford an oppor-tunity for measuring several generations of German spiritual and political history. The verdict is, of course, "weighed and found wanting."

The novel spans fifty-one years, from September 30, 1907, when Heinrich Faehmel successfully enters the architectural competition for the Benedictine Abbey of St. Anthony, to Sep-tember 6, 1958, his birthday at a time when the Abbey has been rebuilt after being destroyed during the war (on the eighty-year-old birthday child's cake sits a replica in frosting). The Abbey itself represents Germany's attempt to hold on to a traditional, agrarian past. Faehmel won first prize with his design:

In the foreground the hamlet of Stehlinger's Grotto, with grazing cows, a freshly dug potato field. . . . And then, in powerful basilican style, the Abbey itself, which I'd boldly modeled after the Romanesque cathedrals, with the cloister low, severe and somber, cells, refectory and library, figure of St. Anthony in the center of the cloister garth. Set off against the cloister the big quadrangle of farm buildings, granaries, barns, coach houses,

own grist mill with bakery, a pretty residence for the steward,
whose job was also to take care of the visitors on pilgrimage.
And there, under high trees, simply tables and chairs at which
to eat a meal, with dry wine, cider or beer, before setting
out on the journey back. . . . Bread for his religious and for the
poor, from grain harvested in his own fields. Yes, there, as an
afterthought, the young architect had added a little room
for the beggars. . . .

For the readers of Böll's *Irisches Tagebuch* (1957), the vision
is the familiar one of a pre-industrial world where poverty is
still sacred, where man has been alienated neither from his
soil nor from his God. But unlike Bernanos and Evelyn Waugh,
who clung romantically to their storybook notion of the Middle Ages, Böll recognizes that beautiful as the life represented
by the Abbey may be, it offers mere escape into the past, not
an excuse for abdication of religious and social responsibility. Father Faehmel looks at his World War I bonds, his two
medals, and his old banknotes, and realizes, too late, that his
life was a failure. He had watched the "Higher Power" coming
in, he had acquiesced in the war, had designed barracks, forti-
fications, and military hospitals. Only his wife Johanna had
dared to blaspheme, had cried, "That fool of a Kaiser." Father
Faehmel had agreed with her, but had refused to take a stand,
saying instead to excuse her revolt that she was pregnant and
had lost two brothers on the battlefield. Now, he can make only
a belated confession: "All along I knew I should have been
saying, 'I agree with my wife, absolutely.' " On his eightieth
birthday, the old man finally summons up the courage to de-
nounce his father's memory and the warrior Germany of his
youth, shouting "Down with the honor of our fathers and our
grandfathers and our great-grandfathers!"

The destroyer of the Abbey is Heinrich's own son, Robert,
the representative of that generation of Germans who grew up
during the Nazi period and faced combat duty in the war
under the epigraph, "Adam where wert thou?" At first glance,

198 Robert's willingness to blow up the Abbey to clear the field of fire between the German and American armies, even though the war was almost over, would seem to symbolize the destruction of the past by the godless present. This, however, is *not* the meaning of Böll's complex religious vision here, as we shall see.

Robert's recollective monologues take him back to a key date in his formative years, the day of "Faehmel's Home Run, July 14, 1935," when he saw one player viciously hitting another with the ball. Robert takes his stand by befriending the victimized Schrella and learns of the relentless persecution suffered by Schrella and his companions, who call themselves "Lambs," who have sworn never to take the "Host of the Beast" to their lips. The Lambs and the Beasts: we are back to that essential split between the hangmen and the crucified which marked Böll's earlier works; more specifically, the Lambs and the Beasts can be said to refer to the anti-Nazis and the Nazis. Not only does Robert take the oath against the Beast; he is also beaten up by the fascistic bully Nettlinger and his crowd. He meets another "Lamb," Schrella's sister Edith, makes love to her, and later marries her, to the embarrassment of his family. Political persecution forces Robert to take refuge abroad until his return is negotiated on the conditions of his taking no part in political activity and his agreeing to immediate induction after completion of examinations. During his brief apprenticeship with the Lambs, Robert had seen others victimized. During the war he remembers constantly those crucified by firing squads or falling bombs: the young anarchist Ferdi Progulske, the waiter Groll, the boy who had slipped messages into the letter box, his wife Edith. It is for them that he blows up the Abbey; the world must accept the truth of evil, not console itself in visions of the past: "He had got himself trained as a demolitions expert, later trained demolition squads himself, implanting formulas which con-

tained exactly what he wanted: dust and rubble and revenge.
. . . A monument for the lambs no one had fed." Implicitly,
Böll is asking whether good can come out of destruction,
whether this deeply motivated gesture is really as noble as
Robert pretends.
The German temperament has often been characterized as
being in perpetual tension between a profoundly destructive
energy and an almost compulsive need for order. Robert's postwar existence is a frightening attempt to replace destruction
with order (and indeed, his father's thousands of breakfasts
with paprika cheese at the Café Kroner reveal a similar need).
Every morning at half-past nine he plays billiards in the Prince
Heinrich Hotel, and the game, reminiscent of his work in demolitions computations, allows him to sublimate his emotions into
mathematical equations: "And the swirl of lines was all angu-
larly bound by geometric law and physics. Energy of the blow
imparted to the ball by cue, plus a little friction, question of
degree, the brain taking note of it, and behold, impulse was
converted into momentary figures." The psychological tension
underlying this attempt at sublimation is clearly unbearable.
With the relaxing assistance of numerous cognacs, Robert confesses his past (especially the secret of the destruction of the
Abbey) to the page boy Hugo, his special guardian angel.
Böll has mixed feelings about priests, as we have seen. Hugo,
the darling of the female clients of the hotel ("Your face is
worth a fortune, pure gold. . . . Why won't you be the Lamb
of God in my new religion?"), becomes the unwitting vehicle
of religious revelation for Robert Faehmel. Hugo is the child-
like confessor who has retained his purity and can therefore
offer absolution. In its complex ritual, the game of billiards
is almost liturgical; the many glasses of cognac seem strangely
sacramental. But the confessor himself confesses, and the story
he tells of his drunken mother, his truancy, and of the constant beatings he received from masters and schoolmates alike

200 (compare the childhood of Bernanos' Curé d'Ambricourt) defines Hugo's symbolic function in *Billiards at Half-Past Nine*:

> "And while they were working me over I used to think, why did
> Christ die, anyway? What good did it ever do me? . . . You
> know what they used to holler at me when they were beating me
> up? *God's little lamb.* That was my nickname. . . . There'd been
> a war a little while before, and they asked me if I'd ever been in
> a cemetery where it said 'Fallen' on the gravestones, the way
> we Germans say it when we mean 'Killed in Battle.' I
> told them, yes, I'd seen 'Fallen.' Then what did I think 'Fallen'
> meant? I said I imagined that the people buried there had
> died from falling down."

"Fallen" has yet another meaning, of course, but Hugo is not
only naive, he is also pure. At the end of the novel, Robert
decides to adopt the fatherless Hugo as his elective son (his
own son Joseph, who is engaged in the reconstruction of the
Abbey, is seen speeding along the Autobahn with his girlfriend
at his side). Novelistically, the adoption seems unsatisfying;
one can only assume it has been placed in the narrative to provide a symbol of Robert's reconciliation with his past guilt, his
acceptance of Christ as a Redeemer, and his realization that
innocence is possible.

Germany cannot forget its past that easily, however: the
spiritual struggle between the crucified and the hangmen continues, will continue. Two key figures from Robert's past are
brought together in a memorable scene: Schrella, whose persecution during the game of rounders had brought Faehmel to
the "Lambs," and Nettlinger, the leader of those who had
partaken of the "Sacrament of the Beast." Schrella was exiled
for most of the Hitler years and has only now returned to
Germany with his name still on the wanted list. He is immediately arrested for suspicious behavior, though Nettlinger's
intercession effects his prompt release from prison (Böll softens
Nettlinger's brutal role in the novel by making him the author
of quite a few charitable actions—he is not a bloodthirsty fa-

natic but a "decent" Nazi, and therefore all the more despicable). Schrella views the new Germany as a girl grown rather fat, with glands working overtime, and married to a rich, hardworking man who has a car and a country house. Nettlinger is the image of the new prosperity: fine Havana cigars, a chauffeur, a taste for good food. In the dining room of the Prince Heinrich Hotel (where his father had been a waiter), Schrella gets his revenge by eating with his hands, reaching across the table and asking to have the leftovers of his chicken dinner wrapped. Symbolically, he is avenged when he, not Nettlinger, wins access to Robert.

The real seer in *Billards at Half-Past Nine* is Johanna Kilb Faehmel, the wife of Heinrich and mother of Robert, though her role as a prophetess of truth is at times blurred by the profusion of internal monologues. It is typical of Böll (and of much recent German literature, as Theodore Ziolkowski has shown in a brilliant article in *Neophilologus*) that Johanna's insights are those of a "madwoman." Her behavior, both political and religious, has always been exemplary, so she is considered insane by her compatriots. In 1917, she spoke out against "that fool of a Kaiser" and tore up a pompous patriotic poem— "Hindenburg! On to the fight!"—which her son had memorized. She gave away her allotments of food from the Abbey farms during both world wars. When, in 1941, she went down to the freight cars to try to go along with the Jews, the time had come to commit her: by then "she was the kind of woman you only see in the old pictures in the museums." To celebrate her husband's eightieth birthday she leaves the asylum, but she cannot be reconciled to the world; when from the hotel room window she witnesses a parade of the "Fighting Veterans League" headed by an official on a white horse, the whole of Germany's warrior past becomes a renewed present in her deranged but clairvoyant mind. She shoots the man on horseback, wounding him slightly. Her shot, like Böll's novel, is a protest against the dechristianized world of the Nettlingers and vet-

202 erans. Throughout the book, we are assaulted by the recurring leitmotif of violence, the bleeding boar hanging in Gretz's butcher shop; Johanna, with Edith, Schrella, Jochen, and Hugo, is the Lamb of God *qui tollis peccata mundi.*

Hans Schnier, the narrator–hero of *The Clown,* is Böll's finest creation. He too is a seeker of truth, an unmasker of hypocrisy, and in his strange, half-mad way, a modern saint. Böll has worked on translations of Salinger's *The Catcher in the Rye* and *Franny & Zooey,* and Holden Caulfield and the clown are spiritual brothers. For Hans Schnier, sincere irreverence is a form of sanctity; the orthodox are uniformly "Christian worms," as he calls the head of the Christian Education Society. His reversal of values is clearly shown in his credo: "I believe that the living are dead, and that the dead live, not the way Protestants and Catholics believe it." The same might have been the credo of the mad Johanna Faehmel. Schnier describes himself as a clown with no church affiliation. His parents, devout Protestants, subscribed to the postwar fashion of denominational tolerance and sent him to a Catholic school. Hans still remembers the hymns, and for a long time he used to sing the *Tantum Ergo* or the *Litany of Loreto* in the bathtub to overcome depressions and headaches. Now alcohol has replaced the hymn: "A clown who takes to drink falls faster than a drunk tile-layer topples off the roof."

As was the case with Robert Faehmel, victimization of the innocent is for Schnier a formative experience. His sister Henrietta happily volunteered for antiaircraft duty as though it were a school outing; she never came back. She had died, her mother explained, "defending Our Sacred German Soil from the Jewish Yankees." The originator of the phrase, the Hitler Youth leader Herbert Kalick, was thereupon denounced as a "Nazi swine" by the eleven-year-old Hans, who was sentenced to dig a tank trap as punishment. From that day on, Hans' parents ceased to exist for him. His entire adult existence as a

clown is a response to a call to unmask the world of prosperous
businessmen and hypocritically pious ladies embodied by his
parents: his father, a wealthy coal merchant whose profits
never diminished, and his mother, now a leading member of
the "Fellowship for the Reconciliation of Racial Differences"
which makes an annual pilgrimage to Anne Frank's House.
Throughout the novel, the image of the sixteen-year-old Henrietta reappears whenever Hans meets the newly crucified victims of West Germany's postwar prosperity.

The central experience in Hans Schnier's twenty-seven-year
itinerary of disillusionment is his "marriage" to Marie Derkum. I use the sacramental term advisedly, because Hans' reversal of values is such that he constantly refers to himself as
monogamous and deplores her "adultery" and "fornication"
with her husband Züpfner: "Prelate Sommerwild is acting the
pimp." Since Hans had become so estranged from his own
parents that he thought of them as running a foster home,
he had put himself under the protection of Mr. Derkum, an
ex-Catholic, a poor, honest man, and worked in his shop. There
he had met and seduced Marie. The consummation of their
love, as Hans remembers it, was a moment of purest innocence.
But Marie has been raised a Catholic, and after traveling
around with the clown for a few years her association with
conventional believers leads her to yearn for a sanctified marriage. Despite numerous miscarriages, Marie worries about
questions of doctrine: Will her children be trained as Catholics? Is she living in sin? Schnier refuses to give in to what he
calls "Catholic blackmail" and denounces the influence of the
Catholic Study Group on his concubine: "Everything was fine
with Marie as long as she was worrying about my own soul,
but you people taught her to worry about her own soul." Marie
runs away to marry the conventional believer Züpfner, to
breathe some "Catholic air." The clown is left alone with his
bottle of brandy and his memories. If he had failed in his career

204 and in his "marriage," his very failure constitutes his purity and makes of him a prophet of truth, an early Christian amid the pagans of the New Germany.

What is a clown? A clown is the messenger of the visionary games of children, the purest form of representational theatre. Hans himself likes only childrens' movies, is as frank and uninhibited as a child, and is always playing his part ("A child, too, never takes time off as a child"). To be a clown is to respond to a *vocatus*, and it is small wonder that Hans' affection for Pope John is explained with touching irreverence: "There was something of a wise old clown about him too, and after all the figure of Harlequin had originated in Bergamo." Above all, the clown, in his act, mirrors the fall of man. Schnier's routines range from his impressions of a bankers' meeting to his own preferred "absurdities of everyday life." During his years of relative success, the clown's function as mirror remained too benevolent; his career depended precisely on those whom he was ridiculing—the wealthy Catholic Pharisees and the complacent businessmen. Despite his poetic gift of detecting odors (usually of corruption) over the telephone, Schnier did not become a real clown until Marie left him. Now, as he explains: "I am a clown and I collect moments." Most of the novel consists of reminiscences of past persecution and of sarcastic telephone appeals for help to those Catholics Schnier most despises. As in most of Böll's works there is in *The Clown* a regular pattern of alternating nostalgia and savage caricature as Schnier struggles toward attainment of his own self-definition: "Neither a Catholic, nor a Protestant, but a Clown." As all his supposed friends desert him, or at best try to force him to take up his conventional career as a public entertainer again, Schnier turns inward toward a most peculiar form of prayer, perhaps a form of madness not unlike Johanna Faehmel's.

Carefully putting on a heavy layer of makeup until the grease cracks, "showing fissures like the face of an excavated

statue," he steps back from the mirror and "looks more deeply
into [himself] and at the same time further away." He picks
up his guitar (Marie and his agent had thought the guitar
undignified) and walks toward the central station. It is Carnival
time and on the station steps a group of "matadors" and
"Spanish donnas" are waiting for a taxi. The clown puts his hat
down beside him and begins to sing:

> Catholic politics in Bonn
> Are no concern of poor Pope John.
> Let them holler, let them go,
> Eeny, meeny, miny, mo.

A stranger drops a nickel into the hat, and the clown goes on
singing. His song is in a perverse way a prayer in praise of
simplicity. Hans Schnier has become a prophetic singer like
the Negro street balladeer in *Acquainted with the Night*. Somehow at Carnival time ("there is no better hiding place for a
professional than among amateurs") people are more genuine
than in their "real," but totally hollow, day-to-day lives. A
faceless, disguised stranger has responded to the song with the
ancient Christian gesture of spontaneous charity. For a brief
moment the hypocrisy of a world where one must pray to
console God yields to the vision of possible harmony contained
in the cacophonic hymn of a nonbeliever. Once again, Böll's
epigraph to a novel (this time from Romans XV: 21) conveys
the essence of his own song: "To whom he was not spoken of,
they shall see: and they that have not heard shall understand."

10 *Maralee Frampton*

Religion and the Modern Novel: A Selected Bibliography

This bibliography has been prepared for readers who may wish to be directed to recent works of criticism in the field of religion and literature. The selections have been limited to those which deal either wholly or partially with spiritual or religious aspects of the modern American, English, and Continental novel. Works on poetry and novels written in the early nineteenth century and before have been excluded. Individual essays from collections will be listed separately if they come under the limitations of this bibliography. One of the most important new additions to criticism in the field is the *Contemporary Writers in Christian Perspective* Series recently published by W. W. B. Eerdmans. This check list makes no pretense of being a complete view of the literature in this vast field; it is a *selection* only.

Abrams, M. H., ed., *Literature and Belief*, New York: Columbia University Press, 1958.
Auden, W. H., "The Christian Tragic Hero," *New York Times Book Review*, Dec. 16, 1945.
Blehl, Vincent Ferrer, S. J., "Literature and Religious Belief," *Comparative Literature Studies*, II, 4 (1965), 303–13.
Brooks, Cleanth, *The Hidden Gods: Studies in Hemingway,*

208   *Faulkner, Yeats, Eliot and Warren*, New Haven: Yale University Press, 1963.

Mr. Brooks lines up literature and Christianity as allies in the fight against materialism.

Chapman, Raymond. *The Ruined Tower*, London: Geoffrey Bles, 1961.

Chase, Richard, "Christian Ideologue," *The Nation*, 170 (Apr. 8, 1950), 330–31.

Connolly, Francis X., "Is a Christian Theory of Literature Possible?," *The McAuley Lectures*, 1961, West Hartford, Conn.: St. Joseph College, 1962.

Contemporary Writers in Christian Perspective Series, Grand Rapids, Michigan: W. W. B. Eerdmans, 1966–67. *Ernest Hemingway*—Nathan A. Scott, Jr. *Flannery O'Connor*—Robert Drake. *Charles Williams*—Mary McDermott Snideler. *Peter DeVries*—Roderick Jellema. *T. S. Eliot*—Neville Braybrooke. *John Updike*—Wesley Kort.

Crossman, Richard, *The God That Failed*, New York: Harper & Row, 1949.

Studies of the reasons for the Communistic leanings of Koestler, Silone, Richard Wright, Gide, Louis Fischer, and Spender.

Cully, Kendig S., "Theology as Literature," *The Christian Century*, LXXXI (Feb. 19, 1964), 237–38.

D'Arcy, Martin C., S. J., "Literature as a Christian Comedy," *The McAuley Lectures*, 1961, West Hartford, Conn.: St. Joseph College, 1962.

Davis, Horton, *The Mirror of the Ministry in Modern Novels*, New York: Oxford University Press, 1959.

Detweiler, Robert, "Christ and the Christ Figure in American Fiction," *The Christian Scholar*, XLVII (Summer 1964), 11–124.

———, *Four Spiritual Crises in Mid-Century American Fiction*, Gainesville: University of Florida Press, 1964.

Studies of the religious aspects of the writing of Styron, 209
Updike, Roth, and Salinger.

Dillistone, F. W., *The Novelist and the Passion Story*, London: Collins, 1960.

Eliot, T. S., "Religion and Literature," in *The New Orpheus: Essays Toward A Christian Poetic*, ed. Nathan A. Scott, Jr., New York: Sheed and Ward, 1964, 223–35.

Elman, Paul, "Holiness and the Literary Mind," *The Christian Century*, LXXVIII (Feb. 22, 1961), 232–33.

———, "Twice-Blessed Enamel Flowers: Reality in Contemporary Fiction," in *The Climate of Faith in Modern Literature*, ed. Nathan A. Scott, Jr., New York: The Seabury Press, 1964, 84–101.

Eversole, Finley, ed., *Christian Faith and the Contemporary Arts*, New York: Abingdon Press, 1962.

Farrell, James T., *Literature and Morality*, New York: The Vanguard Press, 1945.

Fiedler, Leslie, A., *No! in Thunder: Essays in Myth and Literature*, Boston: Beacon Press, 1960.

Fowlie, Wallace. "Catholic Orientation in Contemporary French Literature," *Spiritual Problems in Contemporary Literature*, ed. Stanley R. Hopper, New York: Harper & Row, 1957, 225–41.

———, *Clowns and Angels: Studies in Modern French Literature*, New York: Sheed and Ward, 1943.

———, *Jacob's Night: The Religious Renascence in France*, New York: Sheed and Ward, 1947.

Fraser, G. S., *The Modern Writer and his World*, London: D. Verschoyle, 1953.

Frye, Roland M., "A Christian Approach to Literature," *The Christian Scholar*, XXXVIII (Dec. 1954), 505–14.

———, ed., *Fifty Years of the American Novel: A Christian Appraisal*, New York: Charles Scribner's Sons, 1953.

———, *Perspective on Man: Literature and the Christian Tradition*, Philadelphia, Pa.: The Westminster Press, 1961.

210 Fuller, Edmund, *Man in Modern Fiction*, New York: Random House, 1958.

Gardiner, Harold C., S. J., ed., *Fifty Years of the American Novel, 1900–1950: A Christian Appraisal*, New York: Charles Scribner's Sons, 1951.

——, *Norms for the Novel*, New York: The American Press, 1953.

Glicksburg, Charles S., *Literature and Religon: A Study in Conflict*, Dallas, Texas: Southern Methodist University Press, 1960.

The theme of this book is how twentieth-century "existential anxiety" enters into the creative core of the writing of our time and how contemporary writers deal with it in their works.

Gregory, Horace, "Mutations of Belief in the Contemporary Novel," in *Spiritual Problems in Contemporary Literature*, ed. Stanley R. Hopper, New York: Harper & Row, 1957. 35–44.

Griffith, Richard, *The Reactionary Revolution: The Catholic Revival in French Literature 1870–1914*, London: Constable, 1966.

Hamm, Victor, "Literature and Morality," *Thought*, XV (1940), 278–81.

Harper, Ralph, "The Dark Night of Sisyphus," in *The Climate of Faith in Modern Literature*, ed. Nathan A. Scott, Jr., New York: The Seabury Press, 1964, 65–83.

Hartt, Julian M., *The Lost Image of Man*, Baton Rouge: Louisiana State University Press, 1963.

Hebblethwaite, Peter, "How Catholic is the Catholic Novel?," *The Times Literary Supplement*, No. 3, 413, July 27, 1967, 678–79.

Hoffman, Frederick J., *The Imagination's New Beginning*, Notre Dame, Ind.: University of Notre Dame Press, 1967. A study of the relationship between religion and modern

literature and the involvements of modern writers with religious thought.

————, "The Religious Crisis in Modern Literature," *Comparative Literature Studies*, III, 3 (1966), 263–71.

Hopper, Stanley Romaine, *The Crisis of Faith*, Nashville: Abingdon-Cokesbury Press, 1944.

————, "The Problem of Moral Isolation in Contemporary Literature," in *Spiritual Problems in Contemporary Literature*, ed. Stanley R. Hopper, New York: Harper & Row, 1957, 153–70.

————, "Reports and Prophecies in the Literature of our Time," *The Christian Scholar*, XL (Dec. 1957), 312–30.

Isaacs, J., *The Assessment of Twentieth-Century Literature*, London: Secker and Warburg, 1951.

Jacobsen, Josephine, "A Catholic Quartet," *The Christian Scholar*, XLVII (Summer 1964), 139–54.
  A Study of Flannery O'Connor, Graham Greene, J. F. Powers, and Muriel Spark.

Jarrett-Kerr, Martin, *Studies in Literature and Belief*, New York: Harper & Row, 1954.

————, "The 491 Pitfalls of the Christian Artist," in *The Climate of Faith in Modern Literature*, ed. Nathan A. Scott, Jr., New York: The Seabury Press, 1964, 177–206.

Kauffman, Walter, *Religion from Tolstoy to Camus*, New York: Harper & Row, 1961.

Killinger, John, *The Failure of Theology in Modern Literature*, New York: Abingdon Press, 1963.

Kort, Wesley, "Recent Fiction and its Religious Implications," *Comparative Literature Studies*, III, 2 (1966), 223–33.

Kreiger, Murray, *The Tragic Vision*, New York: Holt, Rinehart, & Winston, 1960.

Krumm, John McGill, "Theology and Literature: The Terms of the Dialogue on the Modern Scene," in *The Climate of Faith in Modern Literature*, ed. Nathan A. Scott Jr., New York: The Seabury Press, 1964, 19–41.

212 Kunkel, Francis L., "Priest as Scapegoat in the Modern Catholic Novel," *Ramparts*, 1 (May 1962), 72–76.

Lewis, R. W. B., *The Picaresque Saint: Representative Figures in Contemporary Fiction.* Philadelphia: Lippincott, 1959. Studies of the characters of Moravia, Camus, Silone, Faulkner, and Greene as combinations of the *picaro* and saint.

Luccock, Halford E., *Contemporary American Literature and Religion*, Chicago: Willett and Clark, 1934.

Ludwig, Jack, *Recent American Novelists*, University of Minnesota Pamphlets on American Writers, Minneapolis: University of Minnesota Press, 1962.

Lynch, William F., "The Theological Imagination," in *The New Orpheus: Essays Toward a Christian Poetic*, ed. Nathan A. Scott, Jr., New York: Sheed and Ward, 1964, 115–38.

————, *Christ and Apollo: The Dimensions of the Literary Imagination*, New York: Sheed and Ward, 1960. A study of two currents running through literature: the one whose symbol is Apollo—its work is the magnificant, the escapist. The other has as its symbol Christ, the Word made flesh—the pursuit of full humanity through a courageous confrontation with the finite, the limited, the real.

Mason, Herbert, "Two Catholic Traditions," *Commonweal*, LXXIV (Sept. 22, 1961), 516–518. A study of the modern Catholic writers of France and America.

May, Rallo, *Symbolism in Religion and Literature*, New York: George Braziller, 1960.

McDonnell, Lawrence V., "The Priest-Hero in the Modern Novel," *Catholic World*, CXLVI (Feb. 1963), 306–11.

McNamara, E., "Prospects of the Catholic Novel," *America*, XCVII (Aug. 17, 1957), 504–64.

Michalson, Carl, ed., *Christianity and the Existentialists*, New York: Charles Scribner's Sons, 1956.

Miller, J. Hillis, "Literature and Religion," *Relations of Liter-* 213
ary Study, ed. James Thorpe, New York: Modern Language
Association of America, 1967, 111–27.

Moeller, Charles, "The Image of Man in Modern European
Literature," in *The New Orpheus: Essays Toward a Chris-
tian Poetic*, ed. Nathan A. Scott, Jr., New York: Sheed and
Ward, 1964, 396–406.

————, *Littérature du XXC siècle et christianisme*, Tournai:
Casterman. Vol. I (*Silence du Dieu:* Camus, Gide, Huxley,
Simone Weil, Graham Greene, Julian Green, Bernanos)
1953; Vol. II (*La Foi en Jésus-Christ*: Sartre, Henry James,
Martin du Gard, Maleque), 1953; Vol. III (*Espoir des
hommes*: Malraux, Kafka, Vercors, Cholokhor, Maulneir,
et al.), 1957; Vol. IV (*L'ésperance en Dieu Notre Père*: Anne
Frank, Unamuno, Marcel, Charles du Box, Fritz Hochwalder,
Charles Péguy), 1960.

————, "Religion et littérature: Esquisse d'une methode de
lecture," *Comparative Literature Studies*, II, 4 (1965),
323–33.

Moseley, Edwin M., *Pseudonyms of Christ in the Modern
Novel*, Pittsburgh, Pa.: University of Pittsburgh Press, 1962.
This study explores the presence of the persistently re-
curring Christ image in modern literature.

————, "Religion and the Literary Genres," *Comparative
Literature Studies*, II, 4 (1965), 335–48.

Mueller, William R., *The Prophetic Voice in Modern Fiction*,
Garden City, N. Y.: Doubleday Anchor Books, 1966.
The major works of Joyce, Camus, Kafka, Faulkner,
Greene, and Silone are interpreted as introductions to the
basic religious doctrines: vocation, the Fall and its fruits,
human and divine judgement, love, suffering, and the
remnant.

Muller, Herbert J., *Modern Fiction: A Study of Values*, New
York: McGraw-Hill, 1937.
Relates the problem of "how to live and what to live for"
in contemporary times. Muller proposes that the contempo-

214   rary significance of many modern writers is "that they have
suggested a means of salvation or at least a route to refuge."
The novelists dealt with are Flaubert, Hemingway, Dreiser,
Conrad, Lawrence, Joyce, Woolf, Proust, Gide, and Mann.

Nicholson, Norman, *Man and Literature*, London: S. C. M.
Press, 1943.

Noon, William T., S. J., "God and Man in Twentieth-Century
Fiction," *Thought*, XXXVII (Spring 1962), 35–56.

Nott, Kathleen, *The Emperor's Clothes*, Bloomington: Indiana University Press, 1954.

    Miss Nott attempts to show the elements of a "pseudo-
religious revival" in modern literature.

Novak, Michael, "Philosophy and Fiction," *The Christian
Scholar*, XLVII (Summer 1964), 100–10.

———, "Prophecy and the Novel," *Commonweal*, LXXVII
(Feb. 22, 1963), 563–69.

O'Conner, Flannery, "The Church and the Fiction Writer,"
America, XCVI (Mar. 30, 1957), 733–35.

O'Donnell, Donat, *Maria Cross: Imaginative Patterns in a
Group of Modern Catholic Writers*, New York: Oxford University Press, 1952.

O'Faolain, Sean, *The Vanishing Hero*, Boston and Toronto:
Atlantic–Little, Brown, 1956.

    Deals with the Catholic novelists Greene, Mauriac, and
Bernanos.

Ong, Walter J., S. J., *The Barbarian Within*, New York:
Macmillan, 1962.

———, *In the Human Grain: Further Explorations of Contemporary Culture*, New York: Macmillan, 1967.

Padovano, Anthony T., *The Estranged God: Modern Man's
Search for Belief*, New York: Sheed and Ward, 1966.

    Discussion of the literary expression of modern man's
values and problems in Kafka, Camus, Salinger, Golding,
and Orwell.

Paton, Alan and Liston Pope, "The Novelist and Christ," *The*

Saturday Review of Literature, XXXVII (Dec. 4, 1954), 15–
16, 56–59.

Pfleger, Karl, *Wrestlers with Christ*, New York: Sheed and
Ward, 1936.

    Studies of the religious psychology of seven modern
writers—Bloy, Peguy, Gide, Chesterton, Dostoyevesky,
Soloviev, and Berdaier.

Pitt, Valerie, *The Writer and the Modern World: A Study in
Literature and Dogma*, New York: Morehouse, 1966.

Ross, Malcolm, "The Writer as Christian," in *The New
Orpheus: Essays Toward A Christian Poetic*, ed. Nathan A.
Scott, Jr., New York: Sheed and Ward, 1964, 83–93.

Savage, D. S., *The Withered Branch: Six Studies in the Modern
Novel*, New York: Pellegrini and Cudahy, n. d.

    Studies of Hemingway, Forster, Virginia Woolf, Margiad
Evans, Aldous Huxley, and Joyce.

Scott, Nathan A., Jr., "Beneath the Hammer of Truth," *Christianity and Crisis*, XVI (Oct. 1956), 124–26.

————, "The Bias of Comedy and the Narrow Escape into
Faith," *The Christian Scholar*, XLIV (Spring 1961), 9–39.

————, *The Broken Center: Studies in the Theological Horizon of Modern Literature*, New Haven: Yale University
Press, 1965.

————, *The Climate of Faith in Modern Literature*, New York:
The Seabury Press, 1964.

    Essays dealing with what is involved in "the whole trans-
action between the Christian Faith and the world of modern
literature."

————, *Forms of Extremity in the Modern Novel*, Richmond,
Va.: John Knox Press, 1965.

    Deals with the theological discrimination found in the
works of Kafka, Hemingway, Camus, and Greene.

————, "The Meaning of the Incarnation for Modern Literature," *Christianity and Crisis*, XVIII (Dec. 9, 1958), 173–75.

216 ——, *Modern Literature and the Religious Frontier*, New York: Harper & Row, 1958.

——, "The Personal Principle in Recent Literature and Its Religious Implication," *Motive*, XV (May 1955).

——, *Rehearsals of Discomposure*, London: John Lehmann, 1952.

An examination of the spiritual and psychological causes of the disinheritance of man in the modern world through the work of four writers: Lawrence, Kafka, Silone, and Eliot.

——, "Religious Symbols in Contemporary Literature," *Religious Symbolism*, ed. Ernest Johnson, New York: Institute for Religious and Social Studies, 1955, 159–84.

——, "The Tragic Vision and the Christian Faith," *The Anglican Theological Review*, XLV (Jan. 1963), 23–25.

Sheed, Wilfrid, "Enemies of Catholic Promise," *Commonweal*, LXXVII (Feb. 22, 1963), 560–63.

Sheppard, Lancelot, *Spiritual Writers in Modern Times*, New York: Hawthorne Books, 1966.

A survey of the spiritual writers of the nineteenth and twentieth centuries.

Sisk, John P., "The Confessional Hero," *Commonweal*, LXXII (May 13, 1960) 167–70.

Slater, John R., *Recent Literature and Religion*, New York: Harper & Row, 1938.

Sonnenfeld, Albert, "Twentieth Century Gothic: Reflections on the Catholic Novel," *The Southern Review*, I, n.s. (Apr. 1965), 388–405.

Spanos, William V., ed., *A Casebook on Existentialism*, New York: Thomas Y. Crowell, 1966.

This book introduces the student to existentialism, its division into three parts includes a section of selections from modern existential literature, general commentary on the content and forms of existential literature, and characteristic statements by the major existential philosophers and theologians of the nineteenth and twentieth centuries.

Spender, Stephen, *The Creative Element*, London: Hamish Hamilton, 1953.
A study of vision, despair, and orthodoxy among some modern writers.

Stewart, Randall, *American Literature and Christian Doctrine*, Baton Rouge: Louisiana State University Press, 1958.

————, "American Literature and the Christian Tradition," published as a "Faculty Paper" by the National Council of the Episcopal Church, 1955.

Stuart, Robert Lee, "The Writer-in-Waiting," *The Christian Century*, LXXXII, (May 19, 1965), 647–48.

Sutcliffe, Denham, "Christian Themes in American Fiction," *The Christian Scholar*, XLIV (Winter 1961), 297–311.

Tate, Allen, "Orthodoxy and the Standard of Literature," *New Republic*, 128 (Jan. 5, 1953), 24–25.

LeSelle, Sallie McFague, *Literature and the Christian Life*, Cambridge: Yale University Press, 1966.
This study argues that there is a legitimate and fruitful relationship between literature and religion.

Trilling, Lionel, "On the Modern Element in Modern Literature," *Partisan Review*, 28 (1961), 9–35.

Turnell, Martin, *Modern Literature and the Christian Faith*, Westminister, Md.: The Newman Press, 1961.

Ulanov, Barry, *Sources and Resources: The Literary Traditions of Christian Humanism*, Westminister, Md.: The Newman Press, 1960.

Vahanian, Gabriel, *Wait Without Idols*, New York: George Braziller, 1964.
Studies of what is religiously decisive in Faulkner, Eliot, Auden, Lagerkvist, and Kafka.

Wilder, Amos N., *Theology and Modern Literature*, Cambridge: Harvard University Press, 1958.

Biographical Notes

ROBERT BOYLE, S. J., is Professor of English at Regis College in Denver. His articles have appeared in *The Modern Schoolman*, *James Joyce Quarterly*, *America*, *Thought*, and other journals. He is the author of *Metaphor in Hopkins* and is currently working on two books—*The Catholic Imagery of Hopkins and Joyce* and a collection of literary essays, *Man is but an Ass*.

ROBERT McAFEE BROWN is Professor of Religion at Stanford University and was a Fulbright scholar in the United Kingdom in 1949–50. He is on the editorial boards of *Theology Today*, *Christianity and Crisis*, and the *Journal of Ecumenical Studies*. His books include *P. T. Forsyth: Prophet for Today*, *The Significance of the Church*, *The Spirit of Protestantism*, *The Ecumenical Revolution*, *Vietnam: Crisis of Conscience* (with Abraham Herschel and Michael Novak). Forthcoming works are *Frontiers for the Church* and *Ecumenical Documents*, the latter with Michael Novak.

A. A. DeVITIS is Associate Professor of English at Purdue University. He is the author of *Graham Greene* and has contributed articles to such journals as *Renascence*, *Twentieth Century Literature*, and *College English*. He has just completed a book on the novels of Anthony Burgess, which is to be published shortly.

MARALEE FRAMPTON, Teaching Fellow in English at the University of Tulsa, is currently completing work towards the Ph.D., with a dissertation entitled "A Reading of Joyce's *Portrait*." She is Assistant Editor of the *James Joyce Quarterly*. Her article "The Anglo-American Critical Reception of Italo Svevo's Fiction" will appear in the forthcoming University of Tulsa *Monograph Six*.

Biographical Notes

HERBERT HOWARTH is Professor of English at the University of Pennsylvania and was a Guggenheim Fellow for the academic year 1966–67. He serves as Advisory Editor to *James Joyce Quarterly* and *Comparative Drama*, and has contributed to *Southern Review*, *University of Toronto Quarterly*, *Mosaic*, and *Comparative Literature*. He is author of *The Irish Writers* and *Notes on some Figures behind T. S. Eliot* and a forthcoming book, *The Tiger's Heart*.

HARRY J. MOONEY, JR., is Associate Professor of English at the University of Pittsburgh, where he teaches Seventeenth Century Literature and Milton. He is on the editorial board of *Milton Studies*, and is at present at work on a book about Milton. Aside from occasional reviews contributed to magazines and journals as diverse as *Commonweal* and *James Joyce Quarterly*, he has published three monographs: *The Fiction and Criticism of Katherine Anne Porter*; *James Gould Cozzens: Novelist of Intellect*; and *Tolstoy: The Epic Vision*.

ALBERT SONNENFELD is currently Professor of French Literature at Princeton University. He has been Visiting Professor at Stanford and Rutgers Universities, and during the academic year 1966–67 was Fulbright Senior Lecturer and Professor of Literature at the University of Reading. Dr. Sonnenfeld is Associate Editor, in charge of literature, of *French Review*, and has published in such journals as *Romantic Review*, *French Studies*, *Southern Review*, and *Novel*. He is the author of *L'Oeuvre poétique de Tristan Corbière*, *Thirty-Six French Poems*, and co-author with E. Sullivan of *Témoins de l'Homme*.

NATHAN A. SCOTT, JR., is Professor and Chairman of Theology and Literature in the Divinity School of the University of Chicago. He is Co-editor of *The Journal of Religion*, and a Fellow of the School of Letters of Indiana University. Among his books are *The Broken Center: Studies in the Theological Horizon of Modern Literature*; *Studies in the Modern Novel*; *Samuel Beckett*; *Albert Camus*; and *Modern Literature and the Religious Frontier*. He has edited *Adversity and Grace: Studies in Recent American Literature*; *The New Orpheus: Essays Toward a Christian Poetic*;

The Climate of Faith in Modern Literature, and numerous other volumes. His new book—*Negative Capability: Studies in the New Literature and the Religious Situation*—will be published in the spring of 1969.

THOMAS F. STALEY is Associate Professor of English at the University of Tulsa. He has been Visiting Professor at the University of Pittsburgh, and during the academic year 1966–67 was a Fulbright Research Professor in Trieste, Italy, where he did research on James Joyce and Italo Svevo. He is Editor of the *James Joyce Quarterly,* Advisory Editor of the University of Tulsa Monograph Series, and on the editorial board of *Twentieth Century Literature.* He has edited *James Joyce Today* and *Essays on Italo Svevo* and has contributed articles on modern literature to *Commonweal, Modern Fiction Studies, Italica,* and other journals both in the United States and Europe. He has books forthcoming on Joyce and on Dorothy Richardson.

WINSTON WEATHERS is Associate Professor of English at the University of Tulsa, and was a Danforth Fellow in 1961. He is the author of two recent monographs—*The Archetype and the Psyche: Essays in World Literature* and *Pär Lagerkvist: A Critical Essay.* He is co-author of two college texts, *The Strategy of Style* and *The Prevalent Forms of Prose,* and has published articles in *Commonweal, ETC: A Review of General Semantics, Southern Humanities Review,* and other journals and literary magazines. His story "The Games That We Played" is reprinted in *Best American Short Stories 1968.*